Maury

The Story of an American Pop Culture Institution

Maury

The Story of an American Pop Culture Institution

by Denise Noe

BearManor Media

2020

Maury: The Story of an American Pop Culture Institution

© 2020 by Denise Noe

All rights reserved.

No portion of this publication may be reproduced, stored, and/or copied electronically (except for academic use as a source), nor transmitted in any form or by any means without the prior written permission of the publisher and/or author.

Published in the United States of America by:

BearManor Media

4700 Millenia Blvd.
Suite 175 PMB 90497
Orlando, FL 32839

bearmanormedia.com

Printed in the United States.

Typesetting and layout by John Teehan

ISBN—978-1-62933-649-7

*Dedicated to my Dad,
Bill E. Dickerson.*

Table of Contents

Chapter 1 1
 The Making of a Man called Maury

Chapter 2 17
 A Talk Show Takes Off

Chapter 3 41
 1998: The Revamped *Maury*

Chapter 4 145
 Behind-the-Scenes Secrets to *Maury*'s Success

Chapter 5 163
 Maury Tragedies… Troubles… and a Toke

Chapter 6 177
 Condemnation and Praise for An American Institution

Bibliography 193

－1－

The Making of a Man Called Maury

Son of a Shirley Man

"I guess I was kind of born to journalism," Maury Povich has observed. It is an apt observation. Maurice Richard Povich was born on January 17, 1939 in Washington, D.C. His dad was famous sportswriter Shirley Povich. His mom was Ethyl Povich. Maury was the middle of three children born into that marriage.

It was indeed fine luck to be the child of the illustrious Shirley Povich. Shirley had been born on July 15, 1905 to Lithuanian Jewish immigrants Nathan and Rosa Povich, owners of a successful furniture store in Bar Harbor, Maine. Shirley was a name mostly given to males during the early 1900s. As an adult, Shirley Povich recalled that, when a child, he had known four other male classmates with the name.

An article by Ralph Berger on the Society for American Baseball Research website states that when Shirley was a youth, he "caddied at the country club in Bar Harbor for two years for Ned McLean, owner of the *Washington Post*. McLean took a liking to Shirley and saw in him a bright and intelligent person. McLean invited Povich to attend his alma mater, Georgetown University, at his expense." When Shirley arrived in Washington, D.C., the already well-experienced caddy caddied for McLean and for President Warren G. Harding.

In 1923, Shirley became a copy boy for *The Washington Post*. Povich called his link with *The Washington Post* "one big love affair" because the newspaper would be such a strong and positive part of his life. Young Shirley Povich learned the newspaper business quickly and soon advanced to police reporter and rewriter. In 1924, he began writing sports stories. Decades later, for an article published in *The Washington Post* in 1995, the elderly Shirley Povich fondly remembered, "I was so excited. My first byline. I could have waited for the page proofs to see it, but I didn't. I went to the composing room downstairs, ran my hands over it on the cold type to make certain it would be there when the paper was printed."

In 1926, he was promoted to sports editor; at 21, he was the youngest sports editor in America. That same auspicious year, he began writing a column entitled "This Morning with Shirley Povich."

A man with a high forehead, long nose, and thin lips, Shirley typically wore his dark hair parted to the side and slicked back. He enjoyed success of a personal nature in 1932 when he married Ethyl Friedman. The couple had met on a blind date.

In 1933, Povich relinquished his job as sports editor to devote more time and energy to his column that had become very popular with the sports-loving segment of the public.

A 1997 *Washington Post* article states that columnist Bob Consodine was both friend and "early Povich protégé." The piece notes that Consodine lauded Povich for possessing "an absolute command over that most formidable of foes, the declarative sentence." An especially poignant example of that command appeared in the Povich column after Lou Gehrig made his July 4, 1939 farewell speech at Yankee Stadium. "I saw strong men weep this afternoon, expressionless umpires swallow hard and emotion pump the hearts of and glaze the eyes of 60,000 baseball fans in Yankee Stadium," Shirley Povich wrote. "Yes, and hard-boiled news photographers clicked their shutters with fingers that trembled a bit."

Another example of that mastery—one with a much happier and brighter tone—appeared after Don Larsen pitched a perfect game in the 1956 World Series: "The million to one shot came through. Hell froze over. A month of Sundays hit the calendar. Don Larsen pitched a no-hit, no-run, no man reached first base in a World Series."

Shirley Povich was an early proponent of ending racism in sports. Berger writes, "in 1941, he went to Florida and watched several Negro League teams. He felt that many were better than many current major league players and many were just as good."

When World War II broke out, Shirley Povich, like the famous Ernie Pyle, became a war correspondent in the South Pacific. Berger states, 'He spent some time with Pyle and was scheduled to accompany him to the island of le Shima in the Okinawa prefecture of Japan, but he broke several ribs due to air-turbulence while flying." Pyle lost his life to a sniper at le Shima.

After reporting on the famous battles of Iwo Jima and Okinawa, Shirley Povich returned to the U.S. at the end of 1945. With World War II over, he went back to covering sports. In 1947, the longtime advocate against racism was gratified to learn that the major leagues signed up the African American Jackie Robinson. "Four hundred and fifty-five years after Columbus eagerly discovered America, major league baseball reluctantly discovered the American Negro," the sports columnist wrote.

The popular sportswriter enjoyed fans among the highest echelons of society. A *Washington Post* article reported that President Dwight D. Eisenhower, who "always insisted *The Post* was too liberal for his taste" said he was "a huge fan of Povich's." Vice-President Richard Nixon told *Post* publisher Phil Graham, "Shirley Povich is the only reason I read your newspaper."

Shirley Povich received many honors throughout his illustrious career. He earned the National Headliners Award in 1947. In 1955, he was President of the Baseball Writers Association of America. In 1957, Povich won the E. P. Dutton Prize. He won the Grantland Rice Award for sports writing in 1964, the J.G. Taylor Spink Award from the Baseball Hall of Fame in 1975, and the Red Smith Award in 1983.

That "Shirley" was transitioning during this period from a name that could be that of a person of either gender to one associated specifically with females was the cause of his receiving a singularly odd honor in 1961: Shirley Povich was included in *Who's Who of American Women*. The error was discovered so he did not make a reappearance in the 1962 volume or any subsequent one.

After Shirley Povich officially retired from *The Washington Post* in 1974, he continued to contribute occasional pieces to that newspaper. In May 1995, *Washington Post* publisher Donald Graham held a special luncheon to honor Povich for the 75th anniversary of his employment at the newspaper.

Photographs of Shirley as a senior citizen show that his hair was gray for many years before turning all-white. In his "seasoned" years, he often wore eyeglasses that were sometimes wire-rimmed and sometimes horn-rimmed. The talented and prolific journalist remained active well into his sunset years and often attended sporting events with wife Ethyl by his side. He enthusiastically described Ethyl as "my favorite girl and a wonderful example to us all." He died of a heart attack on June 4, 1998, just a few weeks shy of what would have been his 93rd birthday, leaving as survivors wife Ethyl, sons David and Maury, and daughter Lynn.

A tribute to Shirley Povich on the National Baseball Hall of Fame website states, "Povich wrote over 15,000 columns during a sports writing career which lasted nearly 75 years, witnessing milestones of baseball history from the Senators one and only World Series championship in 1924 to the game in which Cal Ripkin passed Lou Gehrig as the record holder for most consecutive games played."

The Perks and Privileges of Growing Up Povich

Shirley Povich's career meant that little Maury Povich attended many athletic events, especially baseball games, as child. Sharing his Dad's interest in sports—as well as his love for them—the blue-eyed and dark-haired kid became "bat boy" for the Washington Senators baseball team.

When Maury was 15, he started assisting sports broadcaster Bob Wolff. "I got coffee, did the statistics, carried the film equipment, and did anything he wanted," Maury Povich recalled.

After Maury had been working for a few months as Wolff's gofer/assistant, Shirley inquired, "So what is your job?"

"I'm an associate producer!" the teenager enthusiastically answered.

"Son, you've got big-shot-itis," the elder man wryly commented. "You are in the right profession."

Journalist Jeryl Brunner wrote, "From that moment on Maury Povich knew television would be his life's work." Povich has readily acknowledged, "I wanted to work in television because you could have big-shot-itis."

Despite his big-shot-itis, the early adulthood of Maurice Richard Povich was characterized by a certain amount of floundering and indecisiveness. *Biography.com* reports,

"He enrolled at the University of Pennsylvania but struggled to focus on his studies, landing on academic probation and even getting kicked out for poor grades at one point." The article continues that, despite his academic setbacks. "Povich eventually graduated from the school at 23." His bachelor's degree was in television journalism—a major well suited to his background, interests, and aptitudes.

Maury On His Own

Slim, 5'11" at his full height, blessed with a handsome face and ingratiating smile, young Maury Povich began his journalism career in the 1960s. The Washington, D.C. radio station WWDC hired him as an assistant publicity writer in 1962—a life-changing year for him in more ways than one as he married Phyllis Minkoff, an attractive woman with a pleasant smile, on August 26, 1962. He was often assigned to street reporting and soon started covering stories about the goings-on of Capitol Hill. He did a story on the return of Air Force One to the area after the 1963 assassination of President John F. Kennedy.

In 1966, Povich made his television news debut as a sportscaster for WTTG-TV in Washington, D.C. In 1967, he became co-host of a mid-day news program called *Panorama*, covering a wide variety of news stories. At the same time as he covered news, he was a sportscaster and weekend anchor for WTTG until he left that network in 1977.

Representatives from Neiman-Marcus, the famous upscale department store chain, occasionally appeared on *Panorama*. "The kick-off of the Christmas catalogue for Neiman-Marcus was always a big event in the markets where there was a Neiman's and the DC store was relatively new," Pam Porter, who worked for Neiman-Marcus, recalled in an interview with this book's author. Povich made a positive impression on Porter who said, "I always found him to be charming and a great host who did everything to make his guest feel comfortable." She speculates that his paternal heritage contributed to *Panorama*'s popularity: "His father, Shirley, was legendary in Washington, D.C. and I suspect the was, in part, why so many people followed *Panorama*. What do they say about the apple not falling far from the tree?"

The next year, 1968, Povich met Connie Chung, the woman who would eventually become his second wife. She would also eventually catapult to fame in her own right as a TV anchor and journalist. At the time the two met, he was an anchor; she wrote copy. It is not known when their relationship turned romantic but Povich would finish out the 1960s married to Phyllis and would stay wed to her until their 1979 divorce.

In the late 1970s-early 1980s, Povich bounced around between jobs. He worked as a news anchor in Chicago and then headed to Los Angeles for a similar gig. He moved north to San Francisco where he worked as a news anchor and talk show host. Then he went to Philadelphia where he filled similar roles. During this time period, Povich covered such history-making events as the previously mentioned assassination of President John F. Kennedy, the assassination of Civil Rights leader Rev. Martin Luther King, Jr., the Vietnam War-era protests against America's involvement in that conflict, and the Watergate scandal that led to the unprecedented resignation of an American President when Richard Nixon stepped down from office to avoid impeachment.

In 1983, it was back at WTTG-TV for another go-round as host of *Panorama*. He also took over as weekend news anchor. In 1984, he married Connie Chung. An article in *American Media* stated that Povich "two-timed" Chung while they dated. The article quotes "an insider" as proclaiming, "Maury has told friends that he cheated on Connie almost the entire time they dated!" The same source stated, "Maury was still licking his wounds when he began dating Connie" a few months after his marriage to Phyllis Minkoff "hit the skids." Thus, even as he fell in love with Chung, he continued being promiscuous because "he didn't want to be tied down to one woman." Eventually, this person related, Chung tired of being one in an endless parade of women sharing Povich's sexual favors and told him it was either marriage or calling it quits. Povich chose marriage. The anonymous source said, "Now Maury swears that once he walked Connie down the aisle, his cheating days were behind him!'

The two of them have an adopted child named Matthew. Povich's career took a boost when he won the 1984 Emmy for Best Coanchor for his work on the *10 O'Clock News* on WTTG-TV.

In 1986, Povich became host of *A Current Affair*. *Biography.com* elaborates, "Initially an experiment on the part of new Fox chief Rupert Murdoch, who was looking for original programming, *A Current Affair* proved a hit by focusing on the tabloid-type fare that legitimate news outlets rejected. Fans were drawn to the twisted stories of the 'Baby M' case and the 'Preppy Murderer.'" Writer Bryan Curtis sees a harbinger of things to come

The Making of a Man Called Maury | 15

in Maury's coverage of "Baby M," commenting, "It's now recognizable as the first *Maury* paternity show." At first, surrogate Mary Beth Whitehead refused to grant Povich an interview. Then he decided, "We could give only her side… We wouldn't have to water it down with the usual he-said/she-said bullshit." By "picking a side," he got the interview on *A Current Affair*. (The "Preppy Murderer" was Robert Chambers Jr. who pled guilty to manslaughter in the death of sometime girlfriend Jennifer Levin.) Povich made a peculiarly astute comment when he remarked that *A Current Affair* had hit the big time when, after the Rev. Jim Bakker-Jessica Hahn sex scandal of 1987, the show competed with *Nightline* for an interview with Hahn. Povich was nominated for a 1989 Emmy for Best Information Series for *A Current Affair* but did not win.

– 2 –
A Talk Show Takes Off

The Maury Povich Show: Following in Phil's Footsteps

1991 proved to be a pivotal year for the already fabulously successful Maury Povich. Povich published a book he co-wrote with journalist Ken Gross entitled *Current Affairs: A Life on the Edge.* He also got his very own program, *The Maury Povich Show,* a daytime television show. A TV promotional ad for the new program featured a relaxed and cheerful Povich discussing his charmed life. "I grew up in the nation's capital, I was the middle kid," Povich fondly reminisces. "My Dad was a sports writer so I love baseball! In fact, I was the batboy for the Washington Senators when I was nine." He reminisces about the start of his journalism career, about marrying and having two children, and then mentions with a whiff of sadness that his first marriage ended in divorce. He continues, "I got hired in Chicago, I got fired in L. A." He tells a warmly humorous story about how he married Connie Chung, by then famous in her own right as a reporter and news anchor. He remembers that she called him and announced, "We can get married now." When Povich asked why, she explained, "Because I found the dress." A voiceover announces, "Beginning September 9th Maury Povich will bring the experiences of a lifetime to one hour of television every weekday." Then the ad goes back to Maury who smilingly proclaims, "I'm as happy as I've ever been in my life."

On September 9, 1991, *The Maury Povich Show* debuted. The program was modeled after *The Phil Donahue Show*, a thought-provoking and spicy daytime TV series in which guests from varied walks of life were interviewed about social and political issues.

The Maury Povich Show was typically bookended by a beginning in which a confident and smiling Maury Povich, attired in a suit and tie, announced that episode's subjects. The programs ended with Povich enthusiastically exclaiming, "Until next time, America!" That sign off bespoke a merging of optimism and bond between host and audience—an audience that was implied to be the population of the United States.

Like its model, the legendary *Phil Donahue Show*, *The Maury Povich Show* featured a potpourri of inspiring stories of people who had overcome adversity, guests discussing a variety of topical subjects, and celebrities chatting about their lives and careers. The show often tackled more than one topic on an episode, devoting separate segments to different stories and guests. For example, on an early show, Povich, soberly attired in a green-brown business suit, told the audience both in-studio and at-home, "Today it's one woman's incredible battle of the bulge." A film clip of the guest was displayed, showing her as an extremely obese, bespectacled woman with long brown hair pulled back from her forehead, sitting barefoot in a large wing-backed chair and wearing a white blouse and dark skirt, seen playing with a small dog in the living room of what appears to be a middle-class home, and then walking out its front door. Povich explained that Diana was so embarrassed by her 600 pounds that she did not want to be seen in public. However, she had already managed the feat of shedding almost 100 pounds by the time she was Povich's guest. Appearing with her on the episode was fitness guru Richard Simmons who assured her she could lose even more pounds so that, in Povich's words, "her husband will once again be able to wrap his arms around her." An image of the perennially boyish fitness instructor, with his familiar head full of blonde curls, wearing a vaguely Christmas-y sweater of red set off with stars of white, appeared on the screen followed by a photograph of the guest when she was only slightly pudgy and her smiling, short-haired husband had no problem putting an arm around her.

After letting everyone know the basic story of the first segment of that episode, Povich went on to describe its second segment. He informed his audience that it would focus on a 12-year-old girl who called the police to accuse her parents of abuse. Across the screen appeared a pre-teen child at a phone. This was followed by a clip of her parents walking down a street, a middle-aged interracial couple, a white woman with long, softly waved brown hair and a black man in white shirt and white pants. Povich said that the parents deny the charges and claim the child was trying to get attention. Povich somberly added, "Now everyone in town thinks they beat their kids." Then the host enthusiastically gushed, "It's all next on *The Maury Povich Show!*"

A very wide range of situations and life experiences were represented on the show. One episode was built around a real-life Rip

Van Winkle, a Canadian woman named Annie Shapiro who had, at the age of 50, suffered a stroke in 1963 that put her in a coma that lasted 29 years! She awakened on her hospital bed in 1992. Along with a newly conscious Annie Shapiro, her husband, Martin Shapiro, and daughter, Shirley Shapiro, appeared on the program. Povich explained that when Ann had first awakened out of a slumber that had lasted a year shy of three decades, she had complained to a nurse of a headache! She had told her husband, "Martin, turn on the TV, I want to watch *I Love Lucy*." There was an especially poignant moment when Povich asked Martin how he had managed to stay with an unconscious wife for so long—often feeding her, washing her, and giving her medicine. "When I stood before the rabbi, I took my vows forever," Martin explained. The segment ended on a note that was warm yet humorous as, after asking for her husband's permission and that permission being granted, Povich danced onstage with Annie Shapiro.

Some episodes could be heartbreakingly sad. A pre-pubescent victim of child sexual abuse, a little girl named Monique, appeared with her mother on *The Maury Povich Show* to relate how her stepfather had committed a grisly series of sex crimes against her. Wearing a beautiful dress of shiny material, Monique told how the man had put hooks into the ceiling of the bedroom he shared with his wife, Monique's mom, and painted the hooks white so his wife would not notice them. The cruel stepfather had hung the child from those hooks and sexually molested her as she swung from the ceiling. "He said he would show me what the hooks were for," Monique recalled. Then her eyes filled with tears as she bitterly added, "And he did." The man was heard, but not seen, on the program as he spoke from his prison cell. He admitted to his horrible crimes. At one point, the little girl crossed her arms and said to her molester, "You did it so you could enjoy yourself at the expense of me and my childhood." The child's eloquence occasioned an outburst of applause from the audience. The abuser had no defense against the youngster's clearly accurate assessment. This episode was more than just sensationalism. Monique explained, "I want other kids to know they should tell" if they are sexually victimized. Indeed, if even one child watched this show and "told," bringing abuse to an end and an abuser to justice, it was more than worth it to broadcast the episode.

An episode warning of the extreme dangers of "huffing," or what Povich recalled "was called sniffing" when he was young, aired. Povich explained this practice as "getting high by inhaling any product which gives you a buzz." He interviewed men who, as teenagers, had gotten high by huffing propane. On one fateful day, a youth lit a cigarette and the propane caught on fire. He appeared on the show, having been burned on over 95% of his body, using a wheelchair and obviously scarred. A friend sat in the audience and when Povich interviewed the other young man, he disclosed that 45% of his body had been burned in the accident. Also sitting on the guest chairs were a grieving couple whose teenaged son had been killed inhaling butane and an expert on the dangers of inhalant abuse.

The notorious crimes of Richard Ramirez, the brutal California serial murderer known as the "Night Stalker," were the focus of another episode. Povich interviewed Ginny Peterson who had lived through a Ramirez attack. When Povich asked her to describe the crime, she recalled, "He entered the bedroom, we argued briefly and he leaned over and shot me through the face." She elaborated that Ramirez had shot her husband in the head. Peterson added that Ramirez was "standing there laughing" at the agony he had inflicted. She went on to tell the audience that, horribly wounded as he was, her courageous husband actually chased Ramirez out of their home!

Then Povich explained to the audience that, a few months previously, he had interviewed Ramirez in his death row cell. An excerpt of that interview was played. "I think most humans have in them the capacity to commit murder," the remorseless multiple murderer opined. "No, we don't, Richard," Povich retorted. Ramirez continued that most "choose not to, not because they are morally superior" but because their "commitments" and "responsibilities" make it too much of a gamble. After that film clip was shown, Povich asked Peterson to respond to the murderer's remarks and she said, "I feel nothing but scorn, disgust, and pity for him." Povich asked how she could feel pity for him and she replied she felt pity "for someone to be that sick." Soon after this, the camera panned to her husband, Chris, who sat with the audience. "That's my hero," she proudly declared.

The Maury Povich Show did a program about the notorious "Manson Murders" that specifically focused on the question of parole for Susan Atkins, an especially infamous associate of the even more infamous Charles Manson. Appearing on the show to argue against parole were Steven Kay, who had assisted Vincent Bugliosi in prosecuting the Tate-LaBianca case, Patti Tate, sister of murdered actress Sharon Tate, Steve Fournier, who had assisted the late Doris Tate—Sharon's mother—in founding a victims' rights organization, and Donald Lee Laisure, who had briefly been married to the imprisoned Susan Atkins. Laisure is quite a character in his own right, a man who habitually wears a Western-style hat and garb, and makes dubious claims to wealth. He has also been married no less than 45 times. Commenting on the number of Laisure's marriages, Povich said, "I feel tired just hearing the number." The only person arguing for Atkins' parole was her attorney, the attractive Deborah Fraser. The latter sounded like a reasonable and intelligent person but must have felt rather lonely and overwhelmed. (Atkins died years later without ever being paroled. Manson also died in prison a few years later.)

People who had risen to special challenges often appeared on the show. Povich interviewed several people who had participated in the grueling Eco-Challenge, a nine-day race in the wilderness of British Columbia in which teams alternately ride horses, hike, raft, and climb over 320 miles. "It's the most dangerous race in the world over mountains and glaciers," Povich declared. He informed the audience that each team consisted of five members and had to include at least one woman. The screen showed people climbing, hiking, and rafting on this extraordinary race. "I just looked at it and I wanted to quit!" Povich cheerfully acknowledged. One of those interviewed on the show, attorney Michelle Blaine, made a point of saying she held onto her femininity: "I wore lipstick the whole race! Only a Texas woman would do that!"

Guests also appeared on the show who faced challenges that were not voluntarily undertaken. In 1991, a family appeared on the show to talk about their baby, Carmen Thomas, a child born without arms or legs—although she has feet—due to a condition called bilateral amelia. The family appeared on the show again six years later, in 1997, when Carmen was seven. The child came onstage in her wheelchair, displaying how she controlled it with her foot and how she had learned to draw within lines with a pencil held in her mouth.

Two foster children, sisters Jennifer and Kathryn, appeared on the program to tell the world that they hoped to be adopted into the same home. In an interview with this author, the adult Kathryn recalled, "Our social worker accompanied Jennifer and I the whole time. She flew with us to New York [and] we stayed at an expensive hotel." The two kids appeared on the show in their own clothes. "We weren't coached from what I remember and everyone was nice," Kathryn Bowers elaborated. "The experience was good. It was a blessing to be able to get our faces and story out there." Did anything come out of their televised plea to be adopted together? "We did get a family that attempted to adopt Jennifer and I all the way from Alaska, but it ended up not working out." As a result, the sisters "aged out of foster care" without ever being adopted. "Jennifer, sadly, passed away at 21 from a seizure," Kathryn reveals. "It was a tough time." Regarding her present life, she adds, "I'm 32 now. I'm married with one biological daughter who's four and my bonus son who's eleven."

The Maury Povich Show also had its share of light-hearted fare. For example, one episode reunited people with childhood and high school sweethearts. An audience member happily commented on liking such "cute" and "romantic" material. Povich's wife, Connie Chung, has a special fondness for this type of episode: "I always cry over the reunion shows, when they bring people together who haven't seen each other in a long time or families that are reunited. I love those shows."

There were shows about friends who had crushes on "just friends" and wanted to initiate romantic relationships. "We've been friends for a while," a curly haired and bespectacled fellow told a female friend with silky brown hair and bright orange lipstick. "I know a lot about you and you know a lot about me. So I was thinking maybe we should go out." He burst out laughing and his friend burst out laughing. The audience applauded the suitor—who applauded himself. Povich wittily commented, "I love you. I think you're terrific. Let me tell you something: If she doesn't go out with you, *I'll* go out with you!"

Two years later, Povich had another, similar episode. As the show began, Povich said, "That woman *didn't* go out with that guy!… He came all the way from Texas, and he's been on our staff for two years!" The guest-turned-employee was in the audience—applauding and smiling just as enthusiastically as he had on the stage two years previously—and briefly stood. Povich added, "How's that? I liked the guest so much, I hired him on my staff!" Then Povich went on to explain that this was another show about folks who wanted to go from pals to romantic partners.

Some shows were unabashedly sexy as well as light-hearted. One such episode focused on twins. First to be introduced as guests were the "Barbi twins," two sexy female identical twins, Shane and Sia. The dynamic duo, who sat on the *Maury* stage with their blonde hair in gloriously cascading waves and their short skirts giving the audience an eyeful of lovely leg, had shot to fame and glory through a nude September 1991 *Playboy* pictorial. The sexy twins had also posed for their very own 1992 Calendar full of sensuous Barbi twin photographs. Povich informed the audience, "In 1989 this billboard on Sunset Boulevard gave motorists whiplash and made feminists furious and for no other reason these twins became instant stars." A few minutes after Povich interviewed the Barbi twins, they were joined onstage by male counterparts, the Poteat twins Phil and John. Also blonde, the handsome hunks showed off their hairless, smoothly muscled chests and discussed their acting and modeling careers. Part of what made this episode special was that the studio audience consisted of many sets of twins! The twins in the audience had dressed in identical outfits for the occasion.

Many celebrities appeared on *The Maury Povich Show*. Luminaries who graced the stage of *The Maury Povich Show* included entertainment industry heavyweights as Kathie Lee Gifford, Kelsey Grammar, Robert DeNiro, Patti LaBelle, Cybill Shepherd, Della Reese, Andy Griffith, Tanya Tucker, Queen Latifah, Vanessa Williams, Chevy Chase, Ellen DeGeneres, Paula Abdul, Cher, Woody Allen, Richard Gere, Jennifer Lopez, and Sylvester Stallone. Political superstar Hillary Clinton appeared on the show no less five times in years 1997 and 1998.

Actress Susan Anton graced the stage of the program in 1993. "Maury and everyone on the show was very nice and professional," Anton told this author. "It was a positive experience."

Sometimes celebrity appearances were combined with trips down memory lane for host and audience. For example, in 1992 *Maury* aired a show in which Kathy Garver and Johnny Whittaker appeared. Garver played teenaged Cissy Davis and Whittaker played little Jody Davis on the beloved sitcom called *Family Affair*. Airing 1966-1971, the series followed the adventures of bachelor Bill Davis (Brian Keith) as he raised the orphaned children of his deceased brother. Davis was assisted in his efforts by butler/housekeeper and sometime child caregiver Mr. Giles French (Sebastian Cabot).

In the years since her youthful *Family Affair* period, Garver has continued as an actor and branched out as a producer, public speaker, and author. Two books she wrote, *The Family Affair Cookbook* (2009) and *Holiday Recipes for a Family Affair* (2019) were published by Bear Manor Media, the same publishing company responsible for this book on *Maury*. She has also written *Surviving Cissy—My Family Affair of Life in Hollywood* (2015) and *X Child Stars—Where Are They Now?* (2016) which were released by Rowman/Littlefield Publishing.

"I was in New York at the time doing another show and a friend set me on to appear on Maury's show," Garver recalled in an interview with the author of this book.

She cherishes warm memories of that single interview. "I enjoyed Maury's interviewing style," she said. "Maury was very warm and engaging both on the show and on the set." Garver found a bond with the host in a common personal matter. "He was very interested in the fact that I had a baby at the age of forty-five as I was about the same age as Connie Chung and she thought she was too old to have a baby," Garver elaborated. "I guess ultimately they decided to adopt. My son is now twenty-eight and a wonderful, thriving young man. I thought it interesting that Maury shared his concerns and personal life with me. And it tightened my already warm bond with him."

Hosting the Soap Opera Update Awards

In 1994, *The Maury Povich Show* hosted the Soap Opera Update Awards. Noted set designer Andrew Baseman created a special set decoration for this episode. "A friend I had worked with previously was one of the producers and thought of me when they were doing a special episode requiring a different look than the usual home base talk show set they used for most other episodes," Baseman told this author.

What did Basemen do to decorate the set for this very special occasion? "I had large copies made of the MVP Awards (the Soap Opera Update Award version of the Oscar!) and used as decorations on the side walls," he answered. "I also filled the stage with multiple flower arrangements, adding bits of color to the vast stage, and large swaged curtains to help frame the set."

The set designer found the experience quite pleasant. "Luckily, everything went smoothly, and the shoot went well," he recalled. "I did meet Maury briefly and he was quite nice and appreciative of the work I did."

Making Music

Background music is probably not something any show's fans are apt to mention as a reason for liking a program. Nonetheless, it is significant as it helps set a program's mood and tone. Spyros Poulos began composing music for *The Maury Povich Show* in 1994. He continued working for the program after it was revamped as *Maury* in 1998 and his music continues to air on the show as of this 2019 writing. "I am one of the core writers for Beach Street Music which is the custom music library that licenses music to the show," Poulos stated in an interview with the author of this book. "Beach Street Music supervises me as a music composer and producer."

For what parts of the show did/does Poulos compose music? "I composed instrumental background music used throughout the show and going to and coming back from commercials, guest walk ins and offs, etc.," he informed this writer. "One of my compositions is used daily for the segment, 'If you want tickets for the *Maury* who…' before or after commercial breaks."

What types of music did Poulos compose for the program? "Instrumental background music in different styles to reflect various emotional contexts," he stated. Of course, as is hardly unusual for TV show music composers, he penned some compositions that did not make it to the *Maury* airwaves. "Not all of the music I have submitted for the show gets used," he observed.

Let There Be Light

The importance of lighting in any theatrical venture is obvious and hard to overstate. With the exception of the blind and visually impaired, people *watch* television.

Curt Ostermann started working as Lighting Director for *The Maury Povich Show* in 1996. He took over that position from David Clark who had died. This author asked Oysterman how he got *The Maury Povich Show* job. "I work for Alan Blacher Associates as a freelancer," Ostermann answered. "Alan is a close friend who I met in 1978. Alan and I have worked on many projects throughout the years. Alan got a job at *Maury* as the

Lighting Designer, and he hired me as Lighting Director." The basic job of a Lighting Director is to design the specific look required for each shot. With help from the rest of the Lighting Department, the Lighting Director sets up and operates lights and accessories.

In the late 1990s, *The Maury Povich Show* (which would have its name shortened during this time period with a revamping) taped approximately 160 episodes per season. The show was put together on Tuesday, Wednesday, and Thursday of August through April. Thus, employees of the program enjoyed four-day weekends and, much like schoolchildren, three-month summer vacations.

– 3 –
1998: The Revamped *Maury*

In the late 1990s, talk shows began getting increasingly "trashy," focusing on guests with wild sex lives and overall "weirdness." Guests appeared to tell wilder and wilder tales of how they were cheating on their significant others or enjoying bizarre lifestyles. There sometimes seemed to be a kind of competition to get the most sensationalistic possible material centering around guests who wanted to go on television to inform the world of their promiscuity.

Of course, the talk show nadir appeared with the change of *The Jerry Springer Show*, which had been a respectable discussion program covering varied issues of the day, into a show in which people routinely threw punches and pulled hair. How *Jerry Springer* changed so dramatically is a story in itself but it appears to have happened in a kind of offhand manner. Some guests spontaneously got into a fistfight on stage and viewers tuned in to see something that was, at the time, quite shocking. Once a few people got into fistfights and hair pulling contests, guests appeared to take for granted that fighting is what makes the show. Thus, it turned into a regular spectacle of "confessions" and "revelations" followed by professional wrestling-style roughhousing. As the guests fight—or fake fight—onstage, the delighted crowd chants, "Jer—ee! Jer—ee!" If anything of any seriousness or substance is said, the crowd chants, "Go to Oprah! Go to Oprah!" *The Jerry Springer Show* descended straight into the gutter, leaving behind even the pretense of being either serious or in any respect helpful to guests or audience. And as it spiraled into grossness, it garnered higher ratings than its decent competitors.

1998: The Revamped *Maury* | 43

How was *The Maury Povich Show* going to compete with the trash that garnered *Jerry Springer* such high ratings? The decision was made to make Povich's show more sensational—but without sinking to the grotesque level of its popular rival.

In 1998, *The Maury Povich Show* re-created itself as the *Maury* that has lasted until today and become an American pop culture institution. The more casual approach could be seen in the way Povich ditched the previously typical suit and tie for attire that was usually turtleneck and jeans or khakis. *Maury* shows since the revamping tend to fall into the following categories: phobic people and treatments for their phobias; secrets—usually sexual—either voluntarily revealed or "exposed" through such means as polygraph tests; wild teens; controlling men and their downtrodden wives; and its most famous sort of episode, the paternity test. It also continues with some of the themes that went into the initial version such as stories of disabled or damaged people overcoming adversity and shows prominently featuring transgendered people.

The revamping of the show means that its guests have become more unpredictable in their actions. One of the results, according to Lighting Director Curt Ostermann, is that his always-challenging job has become even more challenging. "The show is unscripted and the guests can go wherever they want, whenever they want," he remarks. "Unlike a scripted show, like a soap opera, there are no actors, and the guests do not hit spikes (tape marks on the floor) where their lighting has been specially created. I have to bring up light wherever the guests decide to run off to. We keep most of the light centered around the host chair and the several guest chairs. If someone runs over to the big TV monitor behind Maury, I have to bring up the lighting in that area. When a guest enters down the stairway, I have to bring up the stairway system. When they exit through the arch, I have to bring up that system. We do not keep all those areas lit all the time, because the white light washes out the colored light on the sets, which the producer wants to be as pure as possible. So most of my job concerns calling up the correct lighting areas that I have previously created, whenever they are needed. I am actually 'directing the light' live, during the taping of the shows, hence 'lighting director.' I sit on the front row of the control room along with the video director and the technical director."

Phobia Freak-outs!

Fears of everyday items can devastate and deform people's lives. *Maury* has had interesting episodes about people with phobias. Guests have appeared who were phobic of such ordinary things as cotton balls, frogs, fish, chewing gum, and flowers. A guest appeared who was frightened of birds. One appeared who had no trouble with our feathered friends in general but was terrified of chickens.

Journalist Anya Wassenberg wrote that the show was criticized as "exploiting the unfortunate" for a 2007 episode about a young lady named Mariah who suffered a phobia of pickles. Wassenberg reported that the show took Mariah "to a pickle factory, where she freaked out in front of the cameras." Indeed, this episode was not unique for the show as it is a regular practice to expose the phobic to the feared object and film the person as they become terrified and hysterical.

Typically, the first part of an episode about irrational fears discusses the phobias of the guests and deliberately confronts them with the items which arouse their terror. The second part of the episode shows them after the phobia has been treated. They can now deal, at least without terror if not in complete comfort, with the things they had so dreaded.

One who appeared on some phobia themed episodes was author, motivational speaker, and hypnotist Boris Cherniak. It was his skills and experience in the last capacity that led executives at *Maury* to want him to treat people with phobias. He is a certified hypnotist and member of several hypnosis guilds. He has hypnotized people in stage performances and on previous television programs. Representatives of *Maury* contacted him about appearing on the show and he readily agreed to appear. Did he have any reservations about being on *Maury*? "I had no reservations about my abilities, but was just uncertain how my presentation would appear on television as I have no control over editing or what happens live," he told this author in an interview. "The show follows a skillfully crafted formula of presentation that engages the viewer to capture their attention. The producers were very helpful in providing information for research beforehand to ensure a successful taping." He elaborated that prior TV experience "prepared me for the fast pace and magic of television tapings."

In a page on his website discussing his *Maury* appearances, Cherniak writes that people who suspect a "set up" are wrong: "They are not actors, just folks with a fear who turned to a TV show to get help." He elaborates that the show accomplishes something very positive, not only for the phobic people who appear on it but for many others similarly afflicted: "Thanks to them, others in the same situation get to find out that they are not alone." Cherniak also writes about how damaging phobias can be. "These people are not only terrified, but the fear is ruining their lives," he states.

How do people with phobias get on *Maury*? "They or their loved ones call the show in response to something like, 'If you have a phobia, call the *Maury* show now,'" Cherniak relates on his website. "The producers respond to hundreds and thousands of these calls and select the most unusual and exciting for the broadcast."

Cherniak told this author that it was unnecessary to test subjects before filming to find out if they were hypnotizable. "Everyone is hypnotizable, some to a higher degree than others," he asserted. "We experience a trance state daily—from driving from point A to point B, unaware consciously of our actions that happen automatically, or it could be as simple as daydreaming or reading a book while visualizing the characters in it."

The experienced hypnotist noted that dealing with phobias is dealing with an extreme case of something that is ultimately universal to humanity. "We all have fears, which is essentially a trance that we create ourselves," he commented. "On top of that list is the fear of public speaking, followed by the fear of death. Jerry Seinfeld has a wonderful quote, 'According to most studies, people's number one fear is public speaking. Number two is death. Death is number two. Does that sound right? This means to the average person, if you go to a funeral, you're better off in the casket than doing the eulogy."

Fears can become extreme when circumstances in an individual's life link something usually harmless with trauma, Cherniak asserts. "Phobias normally stem from an incident where a fear is associated with a reaction, or we emulate reactions to a fear by an authority figure," Cherniak told this author. "Chances are that if you saw your mother jump on top of a chair when she saw a mouse, so would you when faced with the same situation. The person often does not remember how the fear came about as they were too young to form those memories. A perfect example of that was when a daughter brought her mother on the show because her mother was scared of 'waterbugs,' only to exhibit the symptoms herself and getting help along with her mother. People with irrational fears and reactions are essentially hypnotizing themselves. A hypnotist breaks the pattern and reprograms the phobic reaction. The process is quick and effective."

Was any problem presented because of the specific phobias the guests on *Maury* suffered? "All phobias are essentially the same," Cherniak answered. "I have dealt with similar fears in the past. The process of eradicating a fear and reaction is based on the principle that we are born fearless and learn how to fear and react. We are ingrained with a fight or flight response and use that knowledge to react when faced with a phobic situation. When removing the fear and reaction, the person is desensitized, such as 'you are an observer and not a participant,' then taken back in time to a moment when they were not scared. It is an NLP (Neuro-linguistic Programming) process called Fast Phobia Cure."

Tapings for episodes about phobias were done in two parts. A beginning part was taped in which Maury Povich discussed the phobic person's fears with him or her and the guest was exposed to the terrifying item either through the showing of pre-taped short films and/or the bringing of the item onto the set. In the case of the person terrified of cotton balls, an actor dressed in a suit filled with cotton balls walked onto the set. The chicken phobic was confronted with a performer wearing a chicken costume. Cherniak told the author, "This is a psychological procedure called 'flooding' or facing your fear in layman's terms." After this "flooding," Boris Cherniak was introduced to the audience and guests. "They followed me to a green room that was already set up with charts to work with them for the next few hours. The process was documented by a videographer, but very little was shown on the air."

While Cherniak worked with the phobic guests, another, completely separate, episode of *Maury* was taped. "When I was done, my subjects were brought back on set to show how well the process worked and they again were faced with whatever terrified them previously."

Luckily for Cherniak, Maury Povich, the *Maury* audience, and, most of all, the phobic guests, all Cherniak's treatments of *Maury* guests were successful. They came back able to approach or touch the item of which they had been frightened without freaking out. Cherniak noted, "The show has therapists available for aftercare and plans in place for a myriad of situations. I was there to help people in need and was successful with my subjects." He continued, "I refer phobia requests to qualified professionals in the person's location, but I prefer performing, empowering, and motivating on the corporate speaking circuit. *Maury* appearances allowed me to help people watching the show who may be in need or unaware that help is available. The show has producers, editors, networks, and directors who follow guidelines of how the audience will see a segment, which I also do not see until it airs."

How did Cherniak prepare for *Maury* appearances? "I have done extensive research on phobias and how they start, grow, and how to eliminate them," he said. "I had numerous meetings with my colleagues, mentors, and teachers to devise the best plan of action in each case, including wording and processes to use."

Did Cherniak's appearances on *Maury* affect his career? "I had appeared on many other TV shows prior to *Maury*," he answered. "It is difficult to judge the full impact and how it affected my career. TV appearances always help boost visibility. Even before *Maury*, I was trusted by producers to deliver the desired effect and ratings every time. *Maury* helped solidify an already stellar reputation."

Deformities and Disabilities: Triumph Over Tragedy

Povich's show often features guests with deformities and disabilities. Such shows emphasize triumph over adversity and guests often make the point that bullies will not stop them from pursuing their dreams and accomplishing their goals. For example, the aforementioned Carmen Thomas, born limbless, appeared on *The Maury Povich Show* twice where she was welcomed enthusiastically by host and audience.

On a *Maury* show, Povich had as his guest a 15-year-old girl named Tishonna who had a condition causing severe facial disfigurement as well as other major medical problems. "She's broken her left leg thirteen times," Tishonna's mother, Tarja, explained.

1998: The Revamped *Maury* | 55

"She's broken her right hip twice. She's broken her neck." Shortly after Tishonna was born, doctors predicted she would never learn to walk or speak—but she learned to do both. "Her condition meant that she went through puberty at age one—at *one*!" Povich exclaimed. "The doctors said she could have gotten pregnant," Tarja said—although that, of course, would have required that the infant be raped.

As host and mother talked, film of Tishonna was shown of her awkwardly but determinedly walking and saying, "Kids at school call me 'E.T.,' 'ugly,' and 'monster.' It hurts my heart."

At the time of Tishonna's *Maury* appearance, she was attending regular school. "What kind of grades does she get?" Povich asked. "Straight A's," Mom proudly answered. Tishonna came onto the stage. The audience applauded their encouragement. Povich said, "You're an inspiration to all of us." Povich chatted some more with the disabled teenager and asked, "Who is your favorite singer?"

"Tweet," Tishonna replied.

"Guess what—Tweet is here," Povich announced. Then Tweet came on stage to sing both to and with Tishonna. Tarja looked on with tears streaming down her face.

One *Maury* episode bore the eloquent title, "Please Don't Stare…We're Not Monsters." Povich introduced a guest named Valerie who had a condition that caused large tumors to grow on her face. "Some people wrongly call it 'Elephant Man's Disease' but it is really neurofibromatosis," Povich explained as a film clip of Valerie played in the background. "She has been treated like a circus freak," Povich elaborated. "She hopes sharing her story will inspire acceptance and understanding." Povich asked the audience, "Welcome this courageous young woman, Valerie." Valerie came onto the stage as the studio audience clapped. She said, "Kids have called me the 'Elephant's Daughter' and 'beast.'" He pointed out that many people have dropped out of school from teasing, but the courageous Valerie graduated from high school. Then her two small children, a little girl with tiny flower decorations in her hair and a little boy in a blue shirt and a decorated button-up blue shirt, were introduced. "They must love you because they've got the biggest smiles," Povich pointed out. Although Valerie said doctors had said it was possible either or both children might develop her disorder, neither showed any sign of it. As Valerie spoke, her son gurgled and made baby talk into a microphone.

Several *Maury* programs about people with disabilities began with the "Bullying Will Not Stop Me…" followed by the guest's name and the word "Story."

"Bullying Will Not Stop Me…Gabe's Story" was the title of one of *Maury*'s most astonishing—and positive—shows. Povich said, "Everybody welcome Gabe to the show!" Not only did the studio audience clap but many of them stood to honor this singularly accomplished individual. The show's guest was none other than Gabe Adams, a man born without either arms or legs who has become an accomplished dancer!

At the start of "Gabe's Story," Povich said, "Look at this video that recently exploded on YouTube." The background film showed twenty-five young ladies dancing and one teen man, Gabe, doing his energetic and accomplished limbless dance. We soon learn that Gabe was adopted into a family that already had thirteen biological children. Background film shows an interview with Gabe talking about the multitude of challenges he faces as a limbless individual and adding, "Bullying made things harder." The film shows how much he has learned to do to manage on his own as Gabe dresses himself, shampoos his hair, brushes his teeth, and writes with an instrument held in his teeth.

Povich interviews Gabe who recalls, "I asked my seventh grade teacher to sign me up for a school talent show.... People were on their feet applauding after they saw me dance."

Despite the verbal slings and arrows of bullying, Gabe got his high school diploma. Povich commented on an ambition of Gabe's that the host believed "spot-on." Gabe explained, "I want to become a motivational speaker."

On a more prosaic level, Povich inquired, "What is the best thing about having thirteen siblings?" "You always have someone to talk with you," the guest replied. "And what is the worst thing?" Povich asked. "Everyone's always talking," Gabe said to the amusement of host and audience.

Gabe Adams was shown dancing onstage with a professional dance troupe called Be Extreme. After the performance, Povich told Gabe, "You did OK, kid."

Povich asked Gabe what he would say to others facing special challenges and getting bullied. "We're all special and unique… Never let anyone tell you that you can't," he answered.

"BWNSM…Courtney's Story" focused on young Courtney Blackmore who was born with cystic hygroma. Povich explained that the condition "causes cysts to grow in her jaw." As a result, her lower face is disproportionate to the rest of her face and she has several medical problems. Povich explained, "Courtney started her own YouTube channel to share her feelings about bullies and sing her favorite songs." A clip is shown from Courtney on her YouTube channel. "Don't bully someone because their life could be ten times harder than yours," she admonishes.

Out came Courtney. "I've had twenty-three major surgeries," she related. "I've been called ugly disgrace and freak." She elaborated that she had often been hit in high school. She was only fifteen years old when she started her YouTube channel.

Povich noted that she has a man in her life. "You're engaged to Chad," Povich exclaimed. "Look at your ring!" The camera showed a close-up of her engagement ring. Then Chad came out to join his ladylove and say he found her "beautiful" and an "inspiration."

The episode ended with Courtney beautifully singing *Fight Song* and bringing the in-studio audience to a standing ovation.

Interviewed by the author of this book, Courtney recalled that she and Chad had a very positive experience with *Maury*. "Our whole episode was amazing," she asserted. "We were all treated with the utmost respect and they were all so sweet and amazing."

Courtney said her appearance tied in with a cause dear to her heart. "I appeared on *Maury* for Bullying Awareness Month," she stated. "They contacted me through my social media. It was all very professional and an amazing experience. They took background film the day we got there and it was super fun."

Did Courtney and Chad have a run-through with Povich prior to actual filming? "There was a big rehearsal for it," she answered. "It made things that much smoother." The couple got the royal treatment—or at least, the TV guest treatment—to look their best on-camera: "The employees did our hair, make-up, and wardrobe!"

What were things like when the cameras were *not* rolling? "Backstage was fun," she remembers. "We would all laugh and just enjoy each other's company."

A close friend of hers enjoyed the privilege of meeting a close friend of the famous Maury Povich: "My service dog got to meet Maury's dog so that was super cute and amazing!"

Courtney Blackmore carries very positive memories of her appearance on *Maury*. "It was all a fantastic experience and I would do it again in a heartbeat," she says.

Help! Someone Looks Awful! *Maury* Makeovers To The Rescue

There are also *Maury* episodes about people who have eye-catching looks not because of something that cannot be helped, like deformity or scarring, but through their own efforts—or lack of effort.

One such episode featured a woman who had been on *Maury* four years previously for a different reason: Danetra feared fiancé Melvin was getting it on with other ladies. Danetra's cousin, Bernard, said he had caught Melvin in suspicious situations. On the *Maury* stage, Danetra dramatically waved around evidence—pieces of female lingerie that were not hers. On came Melvin to deny any two-timing. The polygraph test showed he had failed questions about his infidelity.

Povich informed the audience that Danetra had broken off with Melvin. She had also fallen into a "deep depression." The audience sympathetically "awwwwwed" at this information. Then Povich revealed that she fought depression with a "sexy" look. On the screen behind the host, we see Danetra showing it all in sexy lingerie—that she is wearing in public places. Her new fiancé, Chad, was first intrigued by her sexy look but he wants her to wear lingerie at home in private for him, not for the whole gawking world. "I love my fiancé," Chad proclaims. "She should look like the classy woman I know she is."

Both Danetra and Chad soon graced the stage. Sure enough, Danetra was garbed in a very revealing black teddy with a bright red number draped over her shoulders. She pranced merrily around the stage as Chad appeared exasperated—yet hopeful. For, as Povich soon reminded everyone, Danetra had agreed to a makeover from the show's "team of experts."

Danetra's next appearance was in the same black and red colors but a much more presentable ensemble consisting of a black pantsuit with a belt that had a shiny belt buckle and a bright red blazer. Her hair, previously dyed blonde, was now a soft chocolate. Chad and Povich beamed at the "classy" appearance Danetra now flaunted.

"I look crusty… I wanna look like a snack!" was the title of another makeover *Maury*. Povich began by interviewing Precious, a woman concerned about a close friend named Sabrina. Precious expressed a great deal of admiration for Sabrina, a domestic violence survivor and single mother of four children who has her own vlog entitled "Simply Being Sabrina." However, as Sabrina herself easily admitted, concern for raising her kids has led her to neglect her appearance and Sabrina acknowledged she had a "crusty" sort of look. Precious hoped a makeover would put "more spunk" into her friend. Appearing onstage in a baggy shirt, she was greeted by Povich who promised transformation through his program's "team of experts." The next time Sabrina appears onstage, she wears a lovely, dark blue off-the-shoulder dress, has silky dark hair she can fling in a sexy manner, and flaunts dangling silver earrings.

Like anything on this show, or any other, a makeover segment may be played for dramatic effect. Someone wrote on Reddit about neighbors who appeared on a *Maury* makeover episode. "While the basic story was true, there was a lot of embellishment," the contributor asserted. "Davlau" continued that the wife wanted her husband to quit his band and change his appearance. Davlau writes that *Maury* employees supplied the lady with "very conservative clothes" for her appearance so there would be an extreme contrast with her husband who appeared a "wild man." He says the staff did some "gentle prompting" and that the couple "felt like they had to be dramatic to get on the show." The couple was on the program for about 15 minutes while Povich asked questions. The husband agreed to change his "wild man" appearance. Davlau elaborated, "The wife had to return the clothes she was given to wear on the show." Davlau added that both said their experience was "fun" and that they "would have done it again in a minute."

Telling Secrets To Your Loved Ones… And The World

As was true on its main rival, *Springer*, the new *Maury* often had guests revealing secrets to their significant others on national television. Also like, *Springer* such *Maury* secrets often concerned infidelity.

A typical instance was that of Douglas who explained that he was on the show to tell his wife, Lacresha, something he had been keeping from her. "I know it's going to break her heart and I just hope it doesn't break up our marriage," he related with sadness and foreboding.

Povich introduced Douglas as a family man "who seems to have the perfect life," that includes a wife, children who "depend on him for everything" and who is "pastor of the local church."

A film clip was then shown of Lacresha recalling how anxious she had been "when I got the call from the *Maury* show, my heart just dropped into the pit of my stomach" because "we never kept secrets from each other."

When the two of them were onstage together, Povich asked Lacresha, "Do you watch my show?"

"Yes, I sure do," she replied.

"I think that you know that when people tell secrets on this show, they're usually not good," Povich observed. Then he told Douglas to reveal the information he had been withholding from his wife. He turned to her and said, "For the last eight or nine months, I've been having an affair." She slapped him in fury and stormed backstage. Tears streamed down her face. Povich brought her back onstage. Douglas informed her that he had been having an affair with her best friend. "Douglas, who do you want to be with?" Povich asked. "I want to be with my wife," he answers. Then she made a revelation of her own: "To be honest, I've been messing with somebody, too." The friend with whom the husband has been committing adultery is backstage. She apologized to Lacresha and they hugged. Povich said, "You all have kids." Lacresha remarked, "He better hope they are his."

This type of show is sensational and titillating—but it also points out certain basic truths of the human condition. Monogamy is not a natural state for human beings of either gender—but jealously comes naturally to both. Thus, monogamy has, in many cultures, evolved as an ideal.

Monogamy is a good ideal because it can bring people into especially strong and deep intimacy while at the same time holding down the spread of sexually transmitted diseases and creating a good environment in which to raise children.

However, since it is not natural, it is an ideal often violated—indeed, perhaps more often violated than observed even by those who hold it dear as an ideal.

Not all secrets concerned infidelity. A 16-year-old girl who had given birth when only 14 came on the show to inform her mother she was once again pregnant. The young lady had tears streaming down her eyes as she told her secret. Hearing it caused her mother to collapse to the floor from her chair and start crying. The situation was indeed difficult as the girl and her mom were already caring for a baby. "We're already struggling," the mother said. "I can't do this." Povich gently informed them that his show would take part of the pressure off by supplying formula and diapers for the coming baby for a year.

There was a telling secrets episode that featured a woman disclosing to the man in her life on *Maury* that she had posed nude in a magazine. There were others who came on with different sorts of revelations. Povich has been frequently been asked why people choose to come on television to discuss such sensitive matters. "I wonder about that," he acknowledges. "Basically, I think, they find that there's a safe place on the show. I offer them that and they unburden themselves. They think that maybe after the show, if there's a lot of the baggage before the show, maybe if it can all come out, they can start again."

Another possibility is that many people are willing to sacrifice privacy and endure psychological pain to experience, however temporarily and even if for negative reasons, fame. This "taste of fame" echoes the line of the late Andy Warhol, "In the future, everyone will be famous for fifteen minutes."

"Lie Detector" Dilemmas

Since so many *Maury* episodes involve so-called "lie detector" tests, it is important to discuss what this machine is—and is not. It is certainly a significant invention. The International League of Polygraph Examiners notes on its website, "The polygraph is considered officially one of the greatest inventions of all time" and elaborates that it "is included in the Encyclopedia Britannica Almanac 2003's list of 325 greatest inventions." The website notes that the Encyclopedia Britannica Almanac "is the oldest continuously published English-language encyclopedia and one of the world's most trusted sources of information" so its judgement must be respected.

Although indisputably an important invention, the common nickname for the polygraph is, as most authorities acknowledge, misleading. The polygraph measures physiological responses—and there is no physiological response specific to lying. However, there is a general tendency for people to experience greater stress when lying than telling the truth so the polygraph, which measure indicators of stress, is commonly called a lie detector. Three physiological responses are measured: heart rate and blood pressure, respiration, and skin conductivity. A blood pressure cuff assesses heart rate and blood pressure; pneumographs wrapped around the subject's chest measure rate and depth of respiration; and electrodes attached to the fingertips report skin conductivity or, in common parlance, sweating.

Typically, "control" or "comparison" questions are asked before "relevant" questions are asked. A paper by the American Psychological Association states, "The control questions are designed to control for the effect of the generally threatening nature of relevant questions. Control questions concern misdeeds that are similar to those being investigated, but refer to the subject's past and are usually broad in scope; for example, 'Have you ever betrayed anyone who trusted you?' A person who is telling the truth is assumed to fear control questions more than relevant questions. This is because control questions are designed to arouse a subject's concern about their past truthfulness, while relevant questions ask about an offense they know they did not commit. A pattern of greater physiological response to relevant questions than to control questions leads to a diagnosis of 'deception.' Greater response to control questions leads to a judgment of non-deception. If no difference is found between relevant and control questions, the test result is considered 'inconclusive.'" An article by Katherine To reports that the "preliminary interview between the polygraph examiner and the examinee" gives the examiner an "opportunity to understand the subject's behaviors and responses to information" and that this is valuable since "an idea of the subject's normal physiological responses" assists in detecting "irregularities if the person lies during the actual test." To continues that the examiner during the actual test will ask "about 10 or 11 questions of which only 3 or 4 are 'relevant' questions" with others being control questions which can be such innocuous inquiries as "Is your name x?" and "Do you live in city y?" To comments that these queries "yield non-lying physiological data and provide reference points for comparisons to the relevant questions."

Polygraphs have value. Studies have shown that their results are far more accurate than chance would have it, meaning that people telling the truth usually are found to be "non-deceptive" and those lying usually are found to be "deceptive." Law enforcement detectives see them as an investigatory tool.

However, polygraphs are anything but foolproof which is why they are generally not allowed as evidence in American courtrooms. It is quite possible for those who are guilty to not have their lies caught by the so-called lie detector. Soviet spy Aldrich Ames passed two polygraphs while he was doing his dirty work. "Green River" serial murderer Gary Ridgeway passed a polygraph in which he claimed innocence. Ridgeway was nailed several years later through the irrefutable science of DNA testing. The truth is that some people, especially psychopaths, are so used to lying that they show no more stress when lying than when telling the truth. Some people can "beat it" by thinking about scary or troubling things when answering control questions and thinking about pleasant things when lying. Another way to fool the lie detector is to keep something sharp, such as a tack, concealed on one's person and push on that during the control questions.

There have been many instances in which truth-tellers were found by polygraph examiners to be lying. A dramatic example of this occurred in the case of Wichita, Kansas murder victim Vicki Wegerle. Her widower, Bill Wegerle, was given a lie detector test by the police—which he failed. Understandably upset, Wegerle hired a polygraph examiner to test him. The polygrapher whom he paid also found that he showed "deception" when he denied murdering his wife. Wegerle was not charged with anything since there was no physical evidence tying him to his wife's murder but the grieving man remained under a cloud of suspicion until it was proven that his wife was a victim of the infamous Dennis Rader, or BTK, a serial murderer who had terrorized Wichita for decades. As To observes, "A truth-teller might recognize that a question has significance" and, as a result, "exhibit the same increased cardiovascular and sweat activity as a liar."

Studies of polygraphs come to wildly different conclusions as to their accuracy. U.S. Attorney General John Ashcroft once stated that the polygraphs used by federal agencies had "an error rate of about 15%"—quite a large error rate. Katherine To reported that there is "credible scientific research" that has found "error rates of 40% or more, only slightly better than flipping a coin to decide if a subject is lying." The International League of Polygraph Examiners cites studies that show far greater accuracy: "Based on twelve separate studies involving 2,174 real cases since 1980, evidence suggests that qualified field polygraph examiners are 98 percent accurate in their overall decisions."

The percentage of accuracy cited by the International League of Polygraph Examiners is identical to that cited by Maury Povich on a radio show called *The Breakfast Club*. Asked about its accuracy, Povich confidently answered, "Ninety-eight!"

"The Lie Detector Determined…" Episode Round-Up

The polygraph examiner for *Maury* is Ralph Barbieri who has attained celebrity status in his own right for his role on the show and who often appears on an episode, usually speaking from a front row position in the audience, to discuss his lie detector findings.

How did polygraph exams become such a major part of *Maury*? "Polygraphs had been done [on television] before the *Maury* show," *Maury* producer Paul Faulhaber points out. However, after first giving a polygraph exam on *Maury*, the show's makers knew they had something. "We tested this couple and he failed the test [questions about infidelity]," Faulhaber remembers. "This raw emotion really spilled out." That "raw emotion" made for genuine drama so the polygraph became a *Maury* staple.

Polygraph episodes tend to be about infidelity but are interestingly variant in particulars.

For example, in his usual avuncular manner, Povich introduced a couple, announcing, "Everyone this is Lisa. This is Lisa's husband Johnathan." In Povich's words, the attractive pair seemed to be "the perfect couple" until a month ago when "a doctor's examination showed that Lisa had a sexually transmitted disease." Lisa was certain she had contracted it from her cheating husband. Johnathan was certain she had contracted it through her own cheating. Both swore they had not had sex with anyone else except for the brief period three years prior during which the couple was separated. "We gave them both lie detector tests," Povich informed the audience.

"I'll read Johnathan's results first," Povich declared. "You were asked if you had sexual intercourse with any of the women you work with. You said, 'no.' The lie detector determined you were telling the truth." Povich went on to say that Johnathan was asked if he had engaged in sex with his ex whom he had dropped off someplace. He had denied it and, Povich read, "The lie detector determined you were telling the truth." Finally, Povich said, "You were asked if you had had sexual intercourse with any woman other than ones Lisa already knows about. You said 'no' and the lie detector determined you were telling the truth." Johnathan looked jubilant.

Then Povich read Lisa's results. When asked if she had ever "knowingly given Johnathan an STD," she had denied it and "the lie detector determined you were telling the truth." Lisa smiled and nodded her head—but her vindication was short-lived. For, when asked if she had engaged in extra-marital sex, other than what her husband already knew about, she had said "no" but, Povich read, "The lie detector determined you were lying." Lisa appeared shocked and outraged.

Standing in the front row of the audience, Barbieri stated, "Johnathan passed his lie detector test with flying colors but Lisa showed major reactions when asked about cheating."

The segment ended with the couple having gone backstage, Lisa still strongly denying any infidelity on her part, and Johnathan indicating he was heading to divorce court.

Another rather typical *Maury* lie detector program revolved around Cindy and Tony, a couple who already had a baby and were planning to marry on Valentine's Day—but only if Tony passed a polygraph to prove his fidelity to Cindy for the past year. The relationship had been in jeopardy since Melissa, a close friend to Cindy, told Cindy that Tony had propositioned her and suggested the two of them check into a motel room for a tryst; Tony stoutly denied the allegation. "Tony has cheated on me in the past and Melissa has lied to me in the past so I don't know what to believe," Cindy acknowledged. She was adamant that the wedding was off if he had even tried to be unfaithful with Melissa or if he had enjoyed sexual relations with former girlfriends or with anyone else at all for that matter within the last year. Povich mentioned that Cindy had heard through the grapevine that he had continued the promiscuity he told her he had abandoned. A film clip was shown of Tony proudly proclaiming, "I'm the most innocent man who has ever been on the *Maury* show!" He said he was certain he would pass the lie detector test and expose Melissa as a fraud.

With Povich, Cindy, Tony, and Melissa all on the stage for the showdown, Povich exclaimed, "We've got two lie detector tests!" He waved around the blue cards on which the polygraph test results are recorded.

Povich began with Melissa's results. "You were asked if Tony suggested renting a motel room so you and he could have sex? You said 'yes' and the lie detector test determined that that was a lie! You were asked if you are trying to sabotage their relationship. You said 'no' and the lie detector determined that that was a lie! You were asked if Tony ever made advances to you. You said 'yes' and the lie detector determined that that was a lie!"

As Povich read the results, Cindy and Melissa screamed at each other while Tony looked happily vindicated.

Ahhhh, but then it was time to read Tony's polygraph results. "You were asked if you propositioned Melissa," Povich said. "You said 'no' and the lie detector determined that you were telling the truth."

Tony's face was full of the joy of vindication; Cindy's joyous expression was a match for his.

But… later: "You were asked if you had any sex with another woman in the past year. You said 'no' and the lie detector determined that was a lie!"

The episode ended with Cindy in tears.

Frequently, if the suspected cheater is male, the female who is his Significant Other has found a lot of telltale evidence such as lingerie, cosmetics, purses, and the like around the house. Producer Christine Ponzi was asked for the "craziest" evidence ever shown on the show and answered, "A weave ponytail a woman found in the toilet that came from a woman the man had been cheating with."

Occasionally an issue will be addressed through a polygraph that lacks that standard daytime talk show ingredient of s-e-x. One such episode began with Povich saying, "Welcome Deja to the show!" An attractive and slender middle-aged woman sat on the stage. She believed that no less than $5,000 had been stolen from her! To make matters worse, all the suspects lived under her own roof! She suspected one of her four kids of absconding with her hard-earned dough. "This is a real life who-done-it," Povich proclaimed. Deja had been saving up for years for a family vacation to Disneyworld. A jug held the funds that must have totaled "at least $2,000" she related. To make matters even worse, a few years before the jug vanished, "tax money" she had in envelopes had disappeared. The envelopes contained $3,000 in cash bringing Deja's total loss to $5,000. The screen shows clips of the four suspects: Deja's 20-year-old daughter Lyna, 19-year-old stepson Malaica, 18-year-old Javorious, and 16-year-old DJ. Povich asked Deja to go down the line of suspects. Could she think of a reason Lyna would betray her so? "I have to suspect everyone," Deja answered. Asked about stepson Malaica, Deja recalled, "He had new clothes and shoes" shortly after the jug filled with money went missing. She continued that Javorious is "flashy" and DJ "is my pretty boy"—qualities that conceivably could have led them to use illegal and immoral means to obtain items that would enhance their images. Each of the young suspects traipsed onto the stage. Each of them expressed dismay at being a suspected thief.

All four had been polygraphed. The two instances, tax money and jug money, will be dealt with separately. Povich reads the results regarding the first. Each young person was asked if he or she stole that money, and each denied. *And* in each case, "The lie detector found that you were telling the truth!" Thus, *Maury* could shed no light on that part of this "real life who-done-it."

Things turn out differently regarding the jug. Three of the suspects were cleared by the polygraph but when Javorious denied stealing, "The lie detector determined that was a lie!"

The suspect did not break down and confess but continued to maintain his innocence. The episode ended on a note of dejection for Deja but also a certain air of confusion as the polygraph results increased the weight of the cloud of suspicion over one of her kids but hardly meant the "beyond a reasonable doubt" standard of proof that would be required for a courtroom verdict of guilty.

Although the validity of polygraph results is heavily disputed by experts of diverse sorts, the producers of *Maury* are certain the audience loves hearing polygraph test results. Trzcinski quotes an unnamed *Maury* producer as saying many episodes would be only "stupidity" were it not for the finding of the "lie detector." Writer Bryan Curtis comments that the polygraph findings take "a segment from an unreasonable conflict to a highly resolvable point of fact."

It just so happens that *Maury* polygraph examiner Ralph Barbieri has his very own "favorite Maury memory." It was an episode in which a married couple named Darren and Michele were on. Darren suspected Michele of cheating. She took a polygraph and Barbieri determined that she was telling the truth when she claimed to have been faithful. Darren made an unprecedented accusation against polygraph examiner Barberi: "The only reason she passed is that she gave oral sex to that lie detector guy Ralph." Barbieri recalled, "Darren accused me of receiving sexual favors from his wife Michele to pass my lie detector test! I couldn't believe it!" He answered the charge on *Maury*, asserting, "I would never compromise my integrity or the show's."

"I was astonished," he later recalled. "At the same time, I thought it was funny."

On the show, Barbieri stood up in the front of the audience and stoutly denied Darren's accusation.

"Are you going to deny this, Ralph?" Povich inquired.

"Oh, yes!" Barbieri emphatically answered.

Darren demanded that Barbieri be given a polygraph to find out if he had accepted sexual favors from Michele to give her a passing grade. Barbieri agreed to take that polygraph. Unbeknownst to Barbieri at the time, *Maury* producers set up hidden cameras to film Barbieri when he was polygraphed. The longtime *Maury* employee denied he had accepted sexual favors to give Michele a favorable result and the polygraph examiner found no evidence of deception.

Darren ended up hugging Barbieri on the show.

Chi-Chi-Chi-Chicken Tetrazzini!

The United States of America is the birthplace of many exquisitely delightful dishes including chicken tetrazzini (there are also versions of tetrazzini made from other main ingredients such as turkey tetrazzini or seafood tetrazzini or spaghetti tetrazzini). Diced chicken is combined with mushroom in a sauce crafted from butter and/or cream as well as cheese. Chicken tetrazzini is flavored with wine or sherry and served over some sort of pasta and garnished with parsley. This savory dish is often topped with cheese, onions, breadcrumbs, almonds or some such combination. It often has a browned crust that adds to its rich scrumptiousness.

But… uh… just what is a description of a meal doing in a book about *Maury*?

It belongs here because an episode that started out as a standard episode about infidelity shot to Internet infamy as the "chicken tetrazzini" show.

A woman named Alycia appeared on *Maury* to complain that Paul, her boyfriend of "four long years," was having an affair with her best friend of seven years, Dominique. "I don't know whether to whup her ass or his!" Alycia exclaimed in exasperation.

Then the episode took an eccentric turn as Alycia said she believed Dominique had won Paul over by "cooking him chicken tetrazzini." Alycia continued that she had always known that "Dominique can cook" and she did not know what was special about Dominique's version of chicken tetrazzini but "Paul love it! He love it!"

Paul had indeed been two-timing and Alycia broke off the romance with Paul and the friendship with Dominique. The prominence given to chicken tetrazzini led to Internet memes and remixes in which Povich was shown saying, "Chi-chi-chicken tetrazzini" and Alycia was excerpted talking about the chicken dish. A T-shirt was created bearing the immortal words: "She seducing my man with the chicken tetrazzini." That same legend was printed on tote bags, hats, (perhaps most appropriately) aprons, and buttons. There was even "pet" clothing made that stated, "She seducing my man with the chicken tetrazzini."

After the episode became an Internet sensation, Alycia and Dominique rekindled their friendship. What's more, both ladies appeared in another episode of *Maury*—one in which they both cooked chicken tetrazzini and their culinary creations were served to the studio audience!

DNA and Polygraph Duo

Some episodes have guests taking polygraph tests *and* DNA tests. In one such episode, Povich opened, Everyone welcome Danesha to the *Maury* show." After the studio audience dutifully applauded Danesha, Povich discussed her story. "Danisha cherishes the life she had built with her boyfriend D'Ante." Not only have they been happily together but the couple has a baby son named Messiah. Povich relates that friction was introduced by neighbor Toccarra who has been informing D'Ante that Daneisha had sex with other men and that Messiah may not be genetically his. Povich inquired, "Do you think Toccarra wants D'Ante?" There was a kind of "uh-huh" reaction from the studio audience.

Daneisha nodded her head and added, "They answered for me." Povich asked if Daneisha is certain D'Ante is the biological father of Messiah. "I'm 1,000% certain!" she confidently replied. Boyfriend D'Ante and neighbor Toccarra came onto the stage.

Povich read the polygraph findings first. "You were asked if, during your relationship with D'Ante, you ever had sexual intercourse with another man. You said 'no' and the lie detector determined that was a lie—at least three men." Povich continued by relating that the polygraph examiner had asked her other infidelity-related questions, including "Did you have sexual intercourse with another man around the time you got pregnant?" Povich said she denied any infidelities at all but the lie detector showed deception. Barbieri stated, "She had significant reactions to cheating throughout the relationship." Daneisha was clearly upset by the lie detector results and D'Ante appeared upset in a different way while Toccarro looked smugly vindicated.

"I'm more interested in whether or not you're the father of Messiah," Povich declared as he took the envelope with the all-important information from the *Maury* employee in the audience front row. Povich announced the results, saying, "When it comes to one-year-old Messiah, D'Ante, you are NOT the father!" As Tocarra gloated and D'Ante looked dismayed, Daneisha ran backstage where she collapsed on the floor.

Another combo show featured a couple with the oddly matching names Shane and Shana. The man and woman had been together for four years and were raising a son, 18-month-old D'Andre, whom Shane suspected was not biologically his. The reason for that suspicion was skin tone: Shane and Shana possessed fair complexions while that of D'Andre was dark. Shana had admitted she had sex with two other men during their four-year long relationship. Shane had heard rumors that they were more infidelities than that ones to which she admitted. He wanted her to take a polygraph to clear up suspicions about her playing the field. He also wanted a DNA test to find out whether or not D'Andra was his genetic child.

"People constantly tell me my son is too dark to be mine," Shane said as tears streamed down his face. "It tears me up.… Sometimes she tells me D'Andre isn't mine but she always takes it back.… Her mom is dark, and her father is dark but she came out white so she says that could be it."

As he typically does, Povich read the results of the polygraph examination first. That test found that she was lying when she claimed no more infidelities than the ones she had already disclosed. "I'm more interested in the results of the paternity test," Povich related before taking that all-important manilla envelope into his hands. He read, "In the case of 18-month-old D'Andre, you are NOT the father!"

Given that the couple had been together for years and a deep emotional father-son bond had formed between Shane and little D'Andre, Povich understandably urged

Shane to be cautious about making immediate changes in his life situation based on those tests. Povich said, "I want my counselor to meet with you and with her."

Controlling Men and their Mistreated Women

Another common *Maury* show type is that of controlling/abusive husbands and boyfriends and the women they mistreat. Such men appear to have either missed out on the feminist movement… or to have over-reacted against it by adopting a kind of iron-fisted and unbending male supremacy. They will make statements like, "It's a man's world!" or "I love her and that's why I control her" or "Women were created to serve men." Sometimes they will cite the Bible as having given man dominion over woman. They often reveal that their fathers and grandfathers taught them, "The man is the head of the family" and that they are teaching their sons the same doctrine. Some men have proudly reported that they make special inspections of the bodies of their women to ensure the women have not been cheating. When brought onto the stage, these men often insult their wives or girlfriends and insult the women in the audience.

For example, Cory proudly discussed controlling his wife, Alexis. "I grew up watching the men in my family control women and that's how I control Alexis. Women will always be beneath men because men are the superior gender," he proclaimed. Unlike some of the controlling males, he eschewed physical violence, stating, "I don't have to use my fists." He continued that he often calls Alexis "a worthless piece of trash" or "a dumb bitch." Cory declared, "I run my house the way Trump runs the country." Before leaving for work each morning, Cory gave Alexis a list of household chores he expected her to perform to perfection—and "perfection" was vital. He likes his steak rare so when he came home to a steak that he found overcooked by his standards, she had to make the whole meal over for him. Then she had to eat a can of beans.

A stickler for good housekeeping, Cory disclosed that he routinely went over furniture with a white glove—and would yell at Alexis if he found so much as "a speck of dirt." He also has clothing rules: "My wife is not allowed to wear anything that doesn't come to her ankles."

Downtrodden Alexis was then brought onto the stage—in an ankle-length dress. Cory objected to her speaking without his express permission. Povich asserted, "She is my guest, this is my show, and my house rules." The host continues that should Cory continue to try to control his wife there, "I will take you off the stage." Not more than a few minutes passed before Cory was required to leave the stage.

"I feel like a slave," Alexis sadly revealed. Indeed, that feeling is understandable. Why has she stayed with him? She loves him, the couple have two children, and "I believe he can change." Povich told her, "This is what I call a sanctuary. You don't have to worry what he thinks of you on this stage."

Another example of controlling male guests was Mike. Povich told the audience that Mike had given a series of quotes to the *Maury* staff reflecting Mike's sex role philosophy. Mike declared, "It was a mistake when we allowed women to vote." Povich pointed out, "That was in 1920, about a hundred years ago." Mike insisted that American experience in the last century bears out his assertion as people are worse off than before females were enfranchised. "Women aren't in the house training the kids," he said. Another Mike quote: "A woman doesn't have the ability to think for herself." When Povich inquired about this statement, Mike said, "When people are married, there should only be one voice in that house."

Still another Mike dictum: "Women who hyphenate their names after marriage are sluts." Mike explained that women traditionally dropped their surnames and took on their husbands because they "gave up their identity and took on the man's identity." Povich had a lady in the audience front row stand up. Then Povich explained, "This is the producer of this show: Gloria Harrison *hyphenated* Hall." Mike was adamant that "she must go along with what I just said."

She did not. "I am far from a slut," she asserted. She then complimented her husband: "My husband is secure enough in himself to let me keep my own identity."

A program began with Povich saying, "Punishment room, naughty girl treatment, cold water torture chamber—these sound like themes from an upcoming horror movie, don't they? But they are punishments my guest Cory inflicts on his wife Lisa." Povich quoted Cory as stating, "The role of a woman is to please her man." A film clip of Cory himself is then shown. Cory says that Lisa must cook his meals perfectly and if her efforts result in cuisine that is less-than-perfect, he breaks the plate and throws the food down and she must eat it off the floor. He puts her in a box he calls the "punishment room" in which she must stay for hours even if she urinates on herself. When they are both sitting on the stage, the obviously sad and despairing Lisa reveals a surprise: she has had divorce papers drawn up. Shown these papers, Cory immediately grabs them from her hands and then rips them up. "Get on your knees!" Cory shouts as he readies a leather belt for punishment. She kneels but Povich jumps in to pull her up. "No, you don't!" Povich exclaims. "You're in my house now." Povich's "house" is an abuse-free zone.

On another program, a couple with the alliterative names Jamie and James appeared. Downtrodden and frightened Jamie cowered as she sat on the *Maury* stage. Povich informed the audience, "She must call him 'King James.' She must bathe him and clip his toenails." If she fails to meet his standards in doing household chores, "King James" chokes her, hits her, and bites her. "God created man first," James point out. "Woman is to serve man and to wait on us hand and foot," James declared. "All women—hail King James! Hail James the Great!"

Once Povich opened an episode as follows: "I want to ask all the woman at home and all the women in my studio audience: Would you put up with a man who dragged you by your hair, makes you brush your teeth with a toilet water soaked toothbrush, and forces you to sleep with dirty baby diapers as your pillow? That is exactly what my guest Colby demands of his girlfriend Alisha who is the mother of his child." Then we go to Colby who stoutly relates, "Alisha must refer to me as Master and Big Papa." He said if his dinner is imperfect, he slams her face into the hot dish. He will lock her out in the freezing cold and not let her back in until she has brushed her teeth with a toothbrush that he urinated on. When the two of them are onstage, Alisha observes, "My son's going to grow up to be just like him." Colby is another man who leaves his woman with a list of chores to perform—and who lets loose with brutal punishment should any of them be imperfectly performed.

Maury episodes about controlling and abusive men show attempts to change their conduct through behavior modification techniques. For example, the men may be transported to a funeral home. A coffin is shown to a man. He sees his woman lying in the coffin as if deceased. This brings home the fact that physical abuse can result in death. An abusive man may be transported to a prison so he can see what the consequences for him could be if he kills the woman or even if the long arm of the law pulls him in for his felonious abuses. A common part of the behavior modification therapy is having the controlling/abusive men experience the tables being turned: they become subjects of control and abuse. Men bark out orders to the men and criticize them harshly should chores not be perfectly performed.

The behavior modification techniques often, although not invariably, seem to work as the previously controlling and abusive men often return to the studio to apologize to their mistreated women and vow to change their ways. Not infrequently, updates about such cases are later broadcast about whether or not such men kept their promises.

Colby and Alisha were a *Maury* success story. Kevin "The Hulk" Washington took Colby to a prison cell where Washington barked out orders at Colby. Confronted by the incredibly muscular and physically intimidating Washington, Colby soon appeared helpless and flustered. Washington ordered Colby to scrub out the cell's toilet with a toothbrush and Colby complied. Then Washington ordered Colby to put it in his mouth. "I can't," a tearful and red-faced Colby replied. At the end of the show, he vowed to change.

He did. *Maury* aired an update with Colby, Alisha, and Kevin "The Hulk" Washington. "I apologize to you," Colby told Povich. "I learned how to treat my queen just like a queen." Indeed, Alisha happily disclosed, "He bought me a new toothbrush." Colby said he will never harm Alisha's toothbrush again. Washington had a big rock in his hand and put it on the stage floor. "If you're perfect, you can hit him with it," Washington told the audience members. Aware of the echo of Jesus and the woman taken in adultery, no one volunteered to clobber the reformed Colby with that rock. Colby expressed gratitude to the program and to Washington. "He changed me," Colby said. Then Povich expressed gratitude to Washington, saying, "Kevin, I think you so much for helping the men who come on this show."

Another success story was "King James" who, along with other controlling and abusive men, changed his attitudes after the show.

These episodes inevitably lead to questions about authenticity. Are these guests really controlling/abusive men and controlled/abused women or are they actors? It seems that they are in fact what they represent themselves as being. *Maury* checks out the stories of its guests—unlike *Springer*—and there are certainly enough of these sorts of couples to keep the episodes going.

Although it seems most of these situations are real, there is a possibility of distortion or exaggeration. A Reddit writer claimed his/her sister appeared on a show and added: "They made it seem like they lived together, and she was his slave. In actuality, they both live with their parents."

Once we accept that these situations are real—or "basically" real—we are still left with why these people appear on the show. Of course, it seems obvious why women who are being controlled and abused reach out for help. But why do the men come on the show, knowing their views are regarded as anathema by Povich himself as well as most of his audience and that they will inevitably be booed and jeered and sharply criticized when they appear? Some of these men may be so committed to the beliefs in which they were raised that they will take any opportunity to share them even in the most hostile of environments.

However, it seems likely that many of these men agree to go on these shows because they sense, at least semi-consciously, that their behavior is not merely "politically incorrect" by contemporary standards but morally wrong and destructive to their relationships. On one such episode, *Maury* counselor Dr. Jeff Gardere speculated, "These guys are here today because they know fundamentally there is something wrong." The abusers also know that behavior change is difficult, very difficult, especially when a person was taught that behavior—or misbehavior—in childhood by trusted and beloved authority figures. There is an even stronger obstacle to positive change when the bad behavior in which they were trained was presented as something ordained by God. These men know they cannot change their behavior on their own and may hope, at a semiconscious or even unconscious level, that the *Maury* show and the professionals who work on these episodes will provide them with therapeutic experiences that will enable them to alter their destructive patterns and replace them with positive patterns.

Of course, appearing on a TV show, even one that enjoys the assistance of legitimate therapists, cannot guarantee positive change. The Reddit writer quoted above claimed "nothing" changed after the couple's appearance as they continued in their "on-again-off-again relationship" and said that their lives were "no different" than before that appearance.

Although change can hardly be guaranteed by an appearance on even a well-meaning talk show, it seems that *some* couples benefit through these appearances. To the extent that *Maury* helps controlling and abusive men lighten up on their negative tendencies, the program not only helps the women in their lives but helps the men themselves. Perhaps even more importantly, the program, by helping such men change, prevents their children from copying negative role models. The show performs an overall social service when it breaks the cycle of abuse.

Gender Benders Baffle

Men and women are different. A famous French saying is, "Viva la difference!" However, they are far more alike than different—a fact that is underscored by the truth that it is possible for a person wearing the clothing of the other gender to, quite frequently, "pass" as a member of that gender.

"Man or Woman?" is the typical title of a *Maury* episode in which genetic women, or women who were born with female genitalia, appear onstage along with people who were born with male genitalia and are either drag queens (men who dress in women's clothing) or transwomen (people born with male genitals who transition through hormones and surgery to become women).

Individuals are wearing fashionable and sexy female attire, often with elaborate or alluring hairdos, and carefully applied makeup. Povich introduces the person by a female name and the "lady" is seen gracefully and confidently sashaying around the stage. Povich asks members of the audience to speculate as the individual's gender of birth/genitalia. The same individual is "for sure" a man according to some and just as certainly a woman according to others.

When the truth is told, there is inevitably a mixture of "I knew it!" and "I can't believe it!" reactions among *Maury* in-studio audience members and it is likely these reactions are echoed by its millions of TV viewers.

Connie Chung has said her husband, unlike so much of his audience, is not fooled. "Maury has told me that he can always tell because he looks at these people's feet," she states, "He says it's always a man when they have big feet."

The extraordinary influence of *Maury* on popular culture can be seen in the way multiple catchphrases have grown out of the show. "That's a man, Maury!" entered the lexicon as a result of the "Man or Woman?" shows. Drag performer Manila Luzon joined forces with a musical group called the AAA Girls to bring out a song entitled *That's A*

1998: The Revamped *Maury* | 109

Man, Maury! Manila Luzon cheekily sings, "He got body/He got face/He got pipes and he got cakes."

These "gender reveal" episodes do not please everyone. Indeed, some people find them offensive. Commenting on these shows, transwoman Kelli Busey writes, "To a cisgender man or woman this may be great fun. To a transgender person who has just started working part time after being unemployed and homeless for 8 months, this is your worst nightmare." Of course, Busey's overall life situation was, as she acknowledges, apt to make her especially thin-skinned. She goes on to make an analogy about persons of varying ethnicities being "in a break room" where they felt "compelled to remain quiet as coworkers bet on a contest if your parents and family were 'Real Americans' by determining if their backs were wet or dry." She acknowledges that some may find the analogy "ridiculous" since, in today's world, "it is expected and required" that people of any ethnic background be accorded respect. Busey is understandably upset that "transgender people do not have that respect yet." Thus, she sees elements of disrespect and transphobia in such *Maury* episodes.

Busey is far from the only person to find bigotry in these "gender reveal" shows. A petition entitled "Stop Exploiting Transgender Women!" appeared at change.org. Started by Kayden H., it was addressed to *The Jerry Springer Show* as well as *Maury*. The petition declares, "For many years, producers of *The Jerry Springer Show* and *The Maury Povich Show* have shamelessly exploited Transgender women on national and international television. **We demand they halt all production and re-airing of episodes that include content related to the exploitation of Transgender individuals.**" After going over issues connected to *Springer*, the petition states, "*The Maury Povich Show* continues to re-air episodes with titles such as 'Man or Woman?' in which cis-gendered and transgendered women are brought out in front of a live audience who calls out 'That's a man!' or 'That's a woman!' judging by her physical or vocal features." The petition states, "These episodes promote stereotypes about Transwomen's appearance and true gender." It also says, "We will not continue to suffer in silence while mainstream media uses our very existence for their amusement, spreading a culture of fear, hate, and violence against us at the very same time."

Wigged Out Wild Kids

One type of episode for which *Maury* is famed—some would say notorious—are those about misbehaving youngsters. Most commonly, they are teenagers. However, *Maury* has done shows about bratty kids who have not even hit their teens. Elementary school-aged children have appeared on the show to boast of their transgressions.

"I'm seven years old and I smoke cigarettes and roll weed," one little boy boasted. "My favorite drink is whiskey!… When my

Mom says I have to go to school, I punch her, kick her, and slap her. When she cries, I laugh in her face. I'm seven and nobody can tell me what to do!"

"I'm nine years old and I dress sexy everywhere I go," a female child declared. "When I grow up, I'm going to be a stripper and make a lot of money." The little girl related that when her Mom remonstrates, "I tell her to shut the fuck up!"

"I'm seven and I like to wear my sexy clothes!" a little girl exclaimed. "I'm dating three boys." When her mother tries to discipline her, the child said, "I slap her around."

Another grade school terror asserted, "I'm seven. I wear short-shorts and bras and the boys love it all. I love to make out with boys!" The kid continued that when her mother attempted discipline, "I took a knife and cut my Mom's chest! She knows better now than to get me PO'd. Mom, you are so stupid!"

"I'm nine years old and I love setting things on fire!" a boy enthusiastically averred. "You make me mad and I'll burn your house down. I like Marlboros and Camel cigarettes."

"I'm nine and my body is so sexy 20-year-old men stare at me," a girl declared. "I drink, I steal, and I smoke."

It must be noted that young children, however "bad" or rebellious, are *children*. Thus, it is important to realize that their transgressions must be viewed with this in mind. What's more, no child has the legal ability to consent to sexual activity. Children who engage in sexual activity with other children must be helped to avoid such activity. Adults who engage in sexual activity with children are guilty of dreadful criminal offenses—regardless of the child's delusions. Those 20-year-old men staring at a child who dresses in a "sexy" manner may actually be staring out of genuine concern or shock. If they stare out of lust, they better not act on it or they could—and justly so—face criminal charges for it.

The majority of "wild kid" *Maury* shows focus on teenagers. This makes sense as teens are notorious for going through "rebellious" stages. It does not follow that "rebellion" is normal as we do not call teenagers who do *not* rebel against adult strictures *ab*normal. Rather, "teen rebellion" is extremely common for a variety of reasons. One is that they are approaching adulthood and have a natural curiosity about the special freedoms granted to adults. They also yearn to take on adult privileges—before being equipped by nature or training to take on adult responsibilities. Thus, underage drinking and smoking are all-too-common—and anything but new. For example, the 1944 motion picture *Youth Aflame* (a favorite film of this author) featured underaged drinking and adult alarm over it.

Sexual feelings and curiosity are inevitable and strong since most people go through puberty ages 12-14. However, they are hardly equipped to deal with the consequences of sexual *activity* at such ages. The most dramatic consequence, pregnancy, can mean a child being raised by another child with a likely future of mental illness and/or criminality.

Wild teens on *Maury* frequently brag about conduct that is distinctly adult—drinking, smoking, and sexual activity—as well as conduct that would be criminal even in an adult. The latter could be activity that is controversially criminal such as the use of illegal drugs or indisputably criminal such as violence.

Episodes often begin with distraught families telling their stories and the teenagers cheerfully sneering at the trouble they have caused. An example began with middle-aged, silky-haired Patricia sitting on the stage, sadness written all over her countenance as Povich explained that she is a "single mother of four" who has "a painful disease called lupus." Povich continued that Patricia's 14-year-old daughter Tiffany "has hit her mom over 100 times!" On one horrible occasion, the teen inflicted injuries on her mother that were so bad Patricia had to be hospitalized. The adolescent also regularly pounds on her brother Angel, 7. Like Mom, brother Angel once had to go to the emergency room because of Tiffany's abuse. He required several stitches to treat his wound. Then pre-recorded tape was shown of a frowning Patricia describing how scared she is of her own daughter. "She has locked me out of the house," Patricia recalled. Another tape was displayed of kid brother Angel saying, "Sometimes she hits me on the arm, sometimes on the neck. Sometimes she takes my arm and swings me around." Violence was not Tiffany's only wrong as she was in the habit of stealing money and jewelry. Finally, Povich revealed that Tiffany is sexually active.

When a tape was displayed of Tiffany speaking, she said, "I hit my mother every day and she cries like a little baby!… Nobody messes with me and gets away with it!" She came onto the stage shouting, "Whatever! Whatever!" as the audience booed and gave her the thumbs-down sign. Povich pointed out that it is especially awful for Tiffany to hit her mother who is already in pain because of her lupus. "I don't care!" the teenager answered. As might be expected, Tiffany's "whatever" and "I don't care" attitudes were as popular with the studio audience as they were with her own distressed family.

Another typical wild teen segment focused on Taylor, 17, whose Mom, Kelly, and older sister, Brittney, were at their wit's ends. Brittney called the show seeking help for the family, especially Taylor. Povich said, "Kelly and Brittney live in fear because of the wild behavior of Taylor who is addicted to pills—it is rumored she takes twelve Xanax at a time—drives while intoxicated, fights, and steals." What's more, Taylor was already herself a Mom. Her child was a planned pregnancy. "When Taylor was 15, she told her Mom she wanted to have a baby," Povich related. "She had 18-month-old Andres." Kelly said, "Taylor has had him in the car without a car seat. When she loses patience with him, she tells him to shut the f—- up." Speaking for herself, Taylor admitted she sometimes "just walks away" from her son when he is crying and she is frustrated with him. However, she insisted she was not sorry she had him: "My son saved my life." Hidden camera film from the green room was shown of Taylor becoming irritated with her son and finally walking away from him instead of just changing his diaper.

A 13-year-old appeared on the show who, in addition to standard misbehaviors, declared to her mother: "You are *my* property!" Povich was understandably sarcastic when he said, "I can't wait to meet this big shot." Another girl of the same age hit her mother so hard in the face that Mom's teeth went through her lip! Teenagers brag about posting sexy pics of themselves on the Internet along with promiscuity, drinking, smoking, drug use, stealing, and fighting.

Perhaps the most cringe-inducing of all are the girls who are in their early teens and *want* to get pregnant. (The author specifies "early" teens to distinguish them from, say, a 19-year-old married young woman who might express a similar desire without necessarily causing consternation.) One larger implication of these shows is that, while much public concern is—justifiably—over "unplanned" pregnancies, the mere fact that a pregnancy was planned does not necessarily mean a child is apt to be born into good circumstances. The 13-year-old who successfully plans her pregnancy is a child raising a child. However, *Maury* frequently features rebellious young ladies, sometimes just barely in their teens, who are determined to have babies. Oddly, they are usually on the worst possible terms with their own mothers—and are unable to realize that, should they become mothers themselves, their children are apt to think as badly of them as they think of their own moms.

Of course, one of the main reasons family members call *Maury* to discuss wild teen behavior is the hope that the show will facilitate behavior change. There are two basic ways the show attempts to help these young people turn their lives around. In one version, a couple of counselors appear on the show to talk sense into their adolescent brains. One counselor is usually an attractive lady who was herself "wild" in her youth. She may be a former prostitute or stripper who is bitterly disillusioned with her former industry. She often tells the young people about how she was almost killed and how their fate may be to be found murdered in an alley, to live their lives in jail, or to succumb to AIDS. The other counselor is often a big burly man who yells things at the kids like, "Do you really think you're BAD?" The rebellious and loud-mouthed teens are often shocked and intimidated into meek silence. The group of youthful miscreants is often herded into a van and driven to a red-light district or a jail. Sometimes they are taken to homeless shelters where they are required to don aprons and help feed the hungry. *Maury* has also had shows in which the mothers of these youthful miscreants pose as if dead in coffins—a behavior modification technique similar to one sometimes used with controlling men who see their mistreated wives and girlfriends in coffins.

Shows typically end with the kids remorseful and often weeping. Vowing to clean up their acts, they are reunited with their moms.

The second version of wild teen reformation is typically called "Teen Boot Camp." The misbehaving adolescents are taken to a facility where burly men in military-style fatigues yell at them as they go into what amounts to basic training. They perform various calisthenics and such chores as hauling big buckets of water and cleaning up areas. Like new recruits, they must say, "Yes, sir!" as they are ordered about. Although these boot camps last for a few days, they are edited down to minutes for the show. As with the first type of reformation, such episodes typically end with the kids and their moms reunited and the teens pledging to change their bad ways.

Povich is convinced these shows do good. He has done follow-ups suggesting that at least some of the changes are lasting. "We give the teens an example of tough love," the talk show host asserts. "Not only do these kids turn their lives around and get on better with their parents, they go to college and are working."

There are a couple of oddities about the wild teen shows, both of which relate to gender. The first is that they almost always feature wild teen girls. Where, one must wonder, are the wild teen boys? Do all adolescent boys lead sedate and saintly lives? Are there no teens of the male gender who misbehave? Of course not. It is more likely that there is something more sensational about the bad behavior of females and that sexism is the reason for the focus on teen girls rather than teen boys.

The second gender oddity is that mothers appear on the show to express concern unaccompanied by fathers. The absence of fathers may reflect a tendency to continue to regard childcare as a female responsibility even in this age of expanding roles for both genders. It could also mean that the wild teen girls on these shows are apt to come from single-mother homes—a possible factor in their destructive behavior.

1998: The Revamped *Maury* | 123

Paternity Tests Get the Gold!

There is an ancient saying, "A wise child knows who his father is." Built into the human condition is the fact that, biologically, one gender impregnates, and the other gender gets pregnant. There are enormous complications that result from these simple biological truths. One is that the female, who bears—literally—the costs of the sex act, *knows* she is a mother when she gives birth. There are many women who become mothers through adoption or stepmothers through marriage but they can only do so because another woman became a biological mother. Thus, motherhood has a firm biological basis.

Fatherhood is another matter. Since males are biologically exempt from the pain and dangers of pregnancy and childbirth, they also lack the certainty that a child is biologically theirs.

Paternity tests are a source of fascination because they expose basic aspects of human nature. It is a truth, albeit an unpleasant one, that monogamy does not come naturally to humans of either gender. Millions of years of natural selection have left our species in quite a pickle. The human male is in a body that is biologically programmed to spread seed; the human female is in a body biologically designed to diversify seed.

Raising children is very difficult. Raising them to be happy and well-adjusted is even more difficult. It is little wonder that mothers want both financial and emotional support from the fathers of their children. Unfortunately, following their biological instincts means they often do not know the identity of those fathers.

It is upon these uncomfortable basic truths of human existence that the most popular *Maury* episodes are based.

A typical paternity test episode starts with Povich introducing a woman who says a particular man is the biological father of her child. Povich will interview her as she tells the story of how the two of them got together and had sex and how the timing is right for

1998: The Revamped *Maury* | 125

him to be the father. A large photograph of the baby will be displayed alongside a photograph of the man. Very frequently, the mom will point to physical similarities in their features.

The next step is for the man to come onto the stage. The audience often boos him as it knows that he denies that he even could be the father or says he is simply uncertain. He points to the photographs and claims a complete lack of resemblance. He will say he "used protection" or that the timing of the relationship was not right or that he knows/believes that she was having sex with others during the time period in question. He may even deny ever engaging in sex with the woman—but this is quite rare. The man and woman often argue back and forth.

Finally, there is the moment of truth. Maury opens a yellow envelope with the results of the previously taken DNA test. He will start the all-important revelation with either "In the case of" or "When it comes to" and then say the child's name followed by either "You ARE the father!" or "You are NOT the father!"

Should it be revealed that the fellow on the stage IS the father, the mother will often dance around the stage in victory. The man may look shocked or dismayed or, in some cases, quite happy. Maury will ask the man if he will do his legal and moral duty by the child and the father will vow to "be there" for his son or daughter. He might apologize to the mother for doubting her word.

When it is revealed that the man is NOT the father, he often dances. The mother may just look sad or shocked or burst into tears or start running toward backstage or even collapse on the floor. In some cases, she will apologize to the man. He might accept her apology. There are episodes in which the man who is found not to be the father will insult the mother and try to verbally rub it in that she was wrong. Maury will usually put a quick stop to that, telling him this is no longer of concern to him. For example, Maury was backstage consoling a weeping woman who found out from a DNA test that she was wrong. The non-father walked in to taunt her and Maury said, "You're out of this now" and told security officers, "Get him out of here!" The non-father may take the opposite tack, forgive the mother, and also attempt to comfort her. Maury often tells her that the show will help her in finding the actual father—and, indeed, many moms come back to the show for multiple paternity tests.

There are several paternity show variations on the one summarized above. Sometimes the woman and man come on the show with the man learning on the show that she has doubts that he is the father. On other shows, a group of men are brought on because the mother believes that one of them is the father but is uncertain as to which one. Another common variation on the paternity test is the man who wants to be the biological father but has been told by the woman that he is not.

Paternity test episodes are the most popular of the program and, as a result, the most common sort of show.

Just who does these all-important and vital paternity tests? The show has always made use of the DNA Diagnostics Center (DDC), an organization that has helped those seeking answers to DNA-related questions since 1995. Its laboratory is located near Cincinnati, Ohio. The company employs over 200 people.

DDC is aware of how its results may change people's lives, both through *Maury* and otherwise, so it takes special precautions to ensure accuracy. Its website describes its use of the DDC Dual Process "wherein each tested party's swabs are divided in two and are tested by two independent teams to ensure accurate results. At each step during the testing process, samples are identified and checked against records, and laboratory directors review the date from each team's testing to see if the results match." DDC does paternity testing for shows other than *Maury* and its website notes that its tests "are legal paternity tests with court-admissible results, so that show participants can use their results

1998: The Revamped *Maury* | 129

for legal reasons such as child support, child custody, inheritance rights, etc."

One thing that helps keep the suspense in these episodes is that Povich as host is always in the dark about the results until he opens up the DDC laboratory results. Thus, Povich is as surprised by the results as his guests.

Indeed, there was one instance in which Povich was genuinely shocked by the DNA results he opened and read. In that case, a woman had confessed to her husband that she had cheated and the twins whom she had birthed might not be biologically his. When Povich read the results, it was learned that one twin was his and the other was not! The host appeared stunned. He later admitted, "I didn't know that was possible." However, the twins were not identical twins—who had twinned from the same fertilized egg—but fraternal twins from two different eggs. As Povich put it, "This is possible if the lady has been busy in the time period when she can get pregnant."

That same situation, the man being the father of one but not the other in a set of fraternal twins, happened a second time on *Maury*. "Science says that's a million-to-one-shot and it's happened twice on our show," Povich observes.

There are some very unusual—and therefore memorable—paternity test shows. Writer Matt Nahum comments in a headline, "The most unnecessary DNA test in the history of the 'Maury Show' is a barrel of laughs to watch unfold." He refers to a white couple in which the woman gave birth to twins who quite clearly have ancestry that is sub-Saharan African. DNA proved that the white man was not the father of the kids.

However, Nahum may be premature in labeling this episode the way he did. Although it turned out that the kids were not sired by their Dad, there is always the possibility that people of white appearance could have African ancestry of which they are unaware.

Nahum may be unaware of a show in which a white woman, Missy, revealed to her black husband that she cheated on him and that their children—neither of whom showed any evidence of African biological heritage—might not be his. Sure enough, DNA revealed that they were not his genetic offspring.

There was also an episode that people like Nahum would have assumed to be "unnecessary"—and turned out to be quite necessary. An African-American married couple were on the show to test the baby that the wife had delivered—a baby with *very* fair skin. "Maury, I am a black man," the husband declared. "That is a white child. Anyone can see that I'm not the father of that child!" The wife denied having sex with any other man. How could she explain the child's appearance? She said she had relatives who were very fair-skinned. "It can happen," she said plaintively. When the couple were together, Povich told the husband, "Your wife says there's no other possibility." "She's lying," the man answered. "Anybody can see that."

Time for the reveal. Povich opened up the envelope and read, "You ARE the father!"

The husband's jaw dropped and his eyes widened. The fair-skinned child—his biological child—was brought to him and placed in his arms while the father gazed around in shock.

Paternity Potpourri

This section will discuss a few of the famous paternity tests to give this book's readers a general flavor of *Maury* DNA episodes.

"This is Jennifer," Maury announced as a clearly distraught young woman sat silently. "If anybody ever felt they made a mistake by saying one wrong thing, Jennifer does—because she is devastated that her husband is now denying their precious two-month-old son Da'Angelo." He elaborated that only three weeks before filming this segment, Jennifer told her husband Jason in the heat of an argument that the baby was not his biological son. The husband is shown in the background. "Since then, her marriage has completely fallen apart," Povich explained. Jason refuses to provide for the child he believes is not his. "Jennifer had to sell her bed to buy formula so the baby could eat," Povich related. A pre-recorded film is then shown of Jennifer recalling, "A few weeks ago we were arguing, and I made the biggest mistake of my life when I told him he wasn't Da'Angelo's father... I just want my husband to know that this is his son and I want to be a happy family again. I'm 100% positive that my husband is the father of my baby." The pre-recording stops and the screen returns to the *Maury* set with Povich talking with Jennifer. At one point, Povich inquires, "Had he ever questioned before whether he is the father?" "Yes," Jennifer answers. "He did?" Povich says. She explains that Jason sees little physical resemblance between himself and Da'Angelo. Jennifer explains that she never cheated so the baby must be Jason's. Then Jason came onto the stage and took a seat beside his wife. "I've been cheated on before and I swore I'd never let it happen again," he said, obviously in anguish. He elaborated that he felt no link to the child, saw none of his features in littles Da'Angelo. Jason continued that he intended to divorce Jennifer if DNA shows he is not the biological father. Povich asked what Jason would do if DNA showed the opposite. "I will make everything right," he answered, continuing that he would apologize to Jennifer and be a real Dad to Da'Angelo. Povich went to the audience front row where a *Maury* employee held the manilla envelope holding the DNA results. Povich returned to his seat and read, "When it comes to two-month-old Da'Angelo, Jason, you are NOT the father!" Jennifer instantly jumped up, ran toward backstage, but collapsed on the floor before getting very far. "Why did you lie?" Jason demanded. Povich ran to comfort Jennifer and told Jason, "She thought you were the father." As Jennifer helplessly sobbed, Povich said, "We'll help you find the father… We'll give you formula to feed that child."

"Everyone welcome Kianna to our show," Povich said, leading the audience to dutiful applause. "Four years ago, Kianna's dream of

1998: The Revamped *Maury* | 135

having a family became a reality when she and her boyfriend James had their first child, Kimmy." Picture of James and Kimmy flash on the screen. Povich says of the child's endearing expression, "Look at that smile."

Trouble erupted when James found a text message on Kianna's phone reading, "Hey, babe, did you ever tell him that she's really mine?" Kianna explains that the text was "sent by an obsessed guy." She adamantly asserts, "James is the one I love. James is the one I chose." James comes onto the stage. "I was happy when I found out she was pregnant," he says. Povich asks if James thinks little Kimmy looks like him. "No, she doesn't look like me, but I've seen the *Maury* show often enough to know a child doesn't have to look like the father to be his," the guest replies. Povich's expression betrays a certain satisfaction at the way this throwaway remark underlines the influence of his program. James promises to stay in Kimmy's life even if there is no biological link but says he will leave Kianna if the DNA test disproves his biological paternity.

Time for the moment of truth and Povich reads, "You are NOT the father!" Kianna falls into tears and James wails, "For three years you've been lying to me!" Povich puts a hand around Kianna's back to try to lend her emotional support. Then he approaches James. To James, Povich gently reminds, "That little girl thinks of you as her father."

Povich and others associated with the program assert that their paternity tests help people. In 2017, *Maury* had a special show in which youths who had been on paternity testing shows as babies appeared. According to Paul Faulhaber, *Maury* executive producer, "We went back to them as grown-ups to tell us what the last 18 years was like knowing their fathers, having them in their lives. For so many kids it changed everything. It put their lives on a whole new trajectory. They have sent us graduation photos."

According to Povich, "A paternity show has the classic Shakespearean themes. There is love. There is lust. There is betrayal. There is conflict. All these Shakespearean themes are crashing together in a paternity test." Povich also believes such a show amounts to "a real soap opera playing in real times, and within 12 minutes, you get a result."

Connie Chung recognizes that these are her husband's "signature shows" and adds that they "actually make me laugh." She observes, "They've become so campy because they're kind of predictable if one thing happens or if the other thing happens."

The statement "You are NOT the father!" really launched as a catchphrase and Internet meme with a show first aired in January 2005. A woman claimed her ex-boyfriend, Andrew, had sired her child. Povich read the DNA results, "You are NOT the father!" and Andrew instantly jumped up from his chair and began exuberantly dancing around the stage. The website *Know Your Meme* reports, "Andrew's breakdance ceremony soon became a subject of parodies, spawning animated GIFs and photoshopped editions on YTMND [an online community called You're The Man, Dog that centered on webpages with popular memes]." The website elaborates, "Andrew's breakdance ceremony has been also featured in the background of the 2011 comedy film *Bridesmaid*." *Know Your Meme* also reports, "Another popular instance features a clip from an episode aired on June 28th, 2010, featuring a guy named Isaac. Upon hearing the result that he is not the biological father, Isaac jumped up from the couch and ran around the stage in circles while performing jazz hands." Indeed, paternity episodes have led to a multitude of Internet memes. *Biography* observes that some of these memes "have been compiled on Tumblr pages like 'The Results Are In' and 'Holy Maury Mother of God.' Some feature the silly dances performed after a guest learns he isn't the father, while others show the host reading the results of a paternity test but delivering an unrelated comment."

The popularity of the paternity tests is underlined by what happens to Povich when people recognize him on the street. If they are of the male gender, they are apt to exclaim, "Hey, Maury, I'm NOT the father!"

Povich believes these shows do a great deal of good—especially for children whose biological fathers are revealed on the program. After all, Chip Crews notes in a *Washington Post* article, "If a father refuses to contribute financially to his child's upbringing, DNA results are a formidable legal weapon."

The show also checks up on the situation after positive paternity reveals. Povich says that the show helps ensure a bio-father has "every opportunity" to become a read "Dad" to his child. Paul Faulhaber explains, "We'll offer them flights to go see their kids if they want to. We'll send them to their kids' house for the holidays. And we won't even air it. We won't even talk about it. We'll just do it. Because we want to give them every fighting chance to make it happen." What's more, Faulhaber adds, in some cases couples who have appeared on the show to determine paternity "get married" after their appearances. Of course, the show cannot always repair a relationship gone wrong. "Some of these guys still hate the women but they're sending child support checks," Faulhaber comments. "And if that's all that they're going to give, it was more than they gave before they came on the show."

A Show That Can Laugh At Itself: The Tangled Taco Bell Triangle

Perhaps one of the most entertaining *Maury* episodes ever was a satirical skit in which it wittily poked fun at itself. This "Social Media Sit Down" was entitled "Is Elijah Cheating on Christine with Tana?"

Heavyset Christine, a stereotypical fast-food restaurant styled cap on her head and a flower in her hair, her plump face sporting a pair of black horn-rimmed spectacles, sat on the stage as Povich recounted the story of her love affair with Elijah. "Eleven months ago, Elijah proposed to Christine with a ring pop at Taco Bell," Povich related as a film clip of Elijah appearing to make the proposal played in the background—and her pulling the "ring pop" out of the food. Povich continues, "What started out in Taco Bell has turned into taco hell!" The reason is that Christine suspects Elijah of two-timing her with another social media personality, Tana, who is shown dressed in a black sexy outfit. In contrast to Christine, Tana is conventionally pretty with a slim figure and waves of blond locks streaming past her shoulders.

A blow-up of a tweet is displayed in the background. "We have the evidence right here," Christine comments. In that display, Tana professes love for Elijah and, instead of spurning her, Christine points out, "He writes 'Power Couple.'"

Povich notes, "There is a video, isn't there?"

"There *is* a video," Christine agrees.

That video shows a quick kiss between Elijah and Tana.

"How did you feel when Elijah first proposed to you?" Povich inquired.

"Since we were in Taco Bell, I felt hungry," she replied.

"Where is the ring?" the host asked

"I have to admit that I did eat it," she answered.

Elijah is shown in the background professing his love for Christine.

"Prove it, bitch!" Christine exclaimed.

Elijah comes out on the stage. He and Povich exchange a comradely hug.

"So now you're cheating with Maury, too!" Christine exclaimed in faux outrage. "You'll hug Maury but you won't hug me!"

"Maury's a good hugger!" Elijah asserted.

Christine expresses doubt that Elijah really wants to marry her.

"I want to spend my life with you for love *and* tax purposes!" he says.

Flouncing her yellow locks, Tana bounces onto the stage. "He was in my bed last night!" Tana proclaims.

Christine suggests that might be because Tana has a better bed. "And I also have your man," Tana stated.

"But I have a better ass!" the heavyset Christine asserted—to the raucous amusement of the studio audience.

Povich merrily waves around a stack of blue cards and states that Elijah took a lie detector test. "You were asked if you had any sexual contact with Tana other than the little buss on the lips we saw," Povich commented. "You said 'no' and the lie detector test determined you were telling the truth!"

Elijah jumped up from his seat and went to Christine. "You see!" he said. "That's just one question," Christine retorted.

"You were asked if you are really in love with Christine. You said 'yes' and the lie detector determined that was a lie!"

"Ohhhhh!" an apparently heartbroken Christine moans.

"You were asked if you really want to marry Christine. You said 'yes' and the lie detector determined that was a lie!"

On to questions about cheating. "You were asked if, since you've been with Christine, you have had any sexual contact with any other woman. You said 'no' and the lie detector determined you were telling the truth!"

"You were asked if, since you've been with Christine, you have had any sexual contact with another other man."

"No," Elijah interjected.

"You said 'no' and the lie detector determined that was a lie!"

"Oh! Oh!" Christine shouted and ran backstage as Elijah followed her shouting, "Baby! Baby!" She flung her heavy body on a couch. She fell off the couch and onto the floor. Elijah seemed to want to hug her as she came to her feet. Then she raced to a restroom. Before going inside that restroom, she asked, "Is this gender inclusive?"

The episode, a satirical episode in which *Maury* courageously and cleverly lampooned itself, ended on that delightfully comical note.

– 4 –
Behind-the-Scenes Secrets to *Maury*'s Success

The *Maury* Audience

A surprisingly important part of *Maury* is the audience that is in the studio while the shows are filmed. Cameras often pan so the television audience can see the in-studio audience which is an active part of the program in their cheering and, yes, their not-infrequent booing.

Actor and model Robert Shearn was in the audience of a *Maury* episode. He has been in the audience of other shows and gives Maury Povich an enthusiastic A+ for his treatment of the in-studio audience. "Out of all the shows I attended, the *Maury* show was the most enjoyable to me because of his friendliness to the crowd," Shearn revealed in an interview with this author. "There were times that I was edited in a lot more than I expected which was really exciting to see when the show aired." The actor and model elaborated, "I went with a group on a bus trip, so the tickets came from the person in charge of the trip. We were sitting in a section at first where the camera couldn't see us. Then a group of people in the middle of the audience seating left and me and two others I was with got selected to be moved and seated in the section—which was the best space to be spotlighted by the cameras on the audience." The episode Shearn viewed was about couples dealing with issues in their relationships. "There was one relationship that had a couple that the woman said she had a child by the guy and the audience thought he was gay and couldn't be the father," Shearn recollects. "It turned out he was the father after the DNA test." He said another relationship was that of an average-height woman and a male dwarf. The man was, in Shearn's words, "really jealous" and believed she was cheating on him with another, more attractive, dwarf. Shearn said the woman "had chatted online a few times" with the other fellow but never actually met him in person.

"I was not paid cash compensation to be in the audience," he recalled. The makers of the show recognize that the in-studio audience is part of the program and act accordingly. "There was someone telling the crowd to react," Shearn states. Although he received no money, he did enjoy a different type of reward for being in the *Maury* audience. "When the show was over we got free pizza from the show for lunch," he says.

Journalist Anya Wassenberg reports that in-studio audience members often spend "long stretches of time waiting backstage" and that they frequently cope with their boredom through the use of chemicals, both legal and not-so-legal, as they have been spotted "openly drinking from their own flasks or enjoying a blunt." What's more, the same people may sit through "two episodes, and on breaks in between, the diners and bars in the vicinity" of the *Maury* studio do a brisk business. Wassenberg notes that audience members hitting the bottle "would certainly explain a lot."

At the Trip Advisor website, someone wrote, "I have a friend who went to a taping.... She thought it was lots of fun." Another Trip Advisor contributor wrote of being a *Maury* audience member: "We arrived at 8:30 a.m. for an 11 a.m. taping. It was freezing and the line was outside." After that person went through security, the destination was "a holding tank" where the writer and others sat and watched *Maury* shows. Spending over an hour in the holding tank was no hardship since there "are vending machines." Then the audience members are led into the studio and told where to sit. The contributor commented, "It's a very small studio, so there isn't a 'bad' seat." Povich comes out to greet the audience members before taping the show. This Trip Advisor writer remarked, "Taping is very fast.… I'm guessing all four segments were done in about an hour. We were out and in the car at about 1:15ish."

In an interview with Emmanuel Ocbazghi, Povich expressed satisfaction in his audience—whether in-studio or at-home—as well as his guests. "I'm very proud that my audience is built of a rainbow coalition," he stated. "We have every kind of ethnicity in our viewership and our guests as well. I'm proud of that because somehow, either through instinct or just through basic human considerations, my guests and my viewers have kind of felt that I was part of their family even though they know and I know that my experience in life is probably nothing that they've gone through." Indeed, it is a safe bet that few of his guests—at least since 1998—were born to wealth and have joined the ranks of the super-wealthy.

Beginning in 2009, *Maury* was filmed at the Rich Forum Theater on Stamford's Atlantic Street. Reporter Liz Skalka noted that "throngs of audience members stretch down the block" on a typical day.

Reenactment Performers

Maury often features reenactments of incidents that either happened or at least were said by someone to have occurred. The program has frequently dealt with sex crimes and sexual harassment within families. Actor Ray DeFeis Sr. told this author, "I was hired as AFTRA talent for a few hours to portray (a caricature) of this perverted uncle that I had no background information on other than the performance notes that I was given by the director." He acted in scenes that were filmed in a New York City studio and never met with Maury.

DeFeis recalls shooting a scene in which "the uncle is watching television as his niece brings him a sandwich" and another in which "the uncle is in the bathroom arranging a small video camera in an empty shaving kit zipper bag to film his niece in the shower unknown to her." He adds, "I believe we shot a scene where the uncle is viewing the video on his camera and making despicable faces showing his pleasure."

The show has sometimes had psychics and others who claim to have had experiences with the supernatural as guests. Actor Sherman Alpert played a ghost in a *Maury* reenactment. "The entire job involved a photographer taking photos of me with bright lights on me," he told this author.

The 3-Part Structure

A typical *Maury* episode is modeled after a three-act play. Trzcinski observes, "Act I centers on someone venting their grievances about a loved one. Act II features the loved one coming on the stage and confronting whoever has a problem with him or her. Act III is what Maury calls the 'truth' and his producers call the 'reveal.'" In Act III, the results of a DNA test may be announced, or the results of a polygraph declared.

Povich sees similarities between his show and the works of the most esteemed writer in Western history. He has commented that *Maury* possesses "all of the classic, Shakespearean themes including love, dislike and pain." It may seem rather arrogant to compare a daytime TV talk show to Shakespeare—and indeed it is. However, Povich is a man who frankly acknowledges his "big-shot-itis."

Is *Maury* Real?... Why Go On *Maury*?

More than once, observers have wondered: Is what appears on *Maury* real? Some commentators believe the similarity of situations and behaviors of guests strongly suggests that the stories are fabricated, and the actions on-stage are coached and/or acted. Wassenberg reported, "In 2007, a woman named

Lashana went public with her story that her own appearance on the show had been entirely faked. She'd appeared on the show a year earlier for the usual paternity test. Lashana claimed that she had contacted Maury's producers and that they had told her to get three men lined up for paternity tests. The only problem was, all three declined to be on the show." Wassenberg continues that Lashana further asserted that she found a man named Anthony who agreed to appear on *Maury* as a possible father and that "the producers came up with a script for them to follow, including Anthony accusing Lashana of being a 'whore' and Lashana crying and raging against him. Her parents backed up the allegations that her appearance had been scripted."

Paul Faulhaber, *Maury* executive producer, says, "People ask me two questions all the time—are these people real and where do you find them? Yes, they're very real. Some of our guests have never left their hometowns and have never experienced something in their lives of such magnitude."

Another *Maury* producer, Christine Ponzi, asserts, "The stories are real. The evidence is real." She adds, "If it wasn't real, our jobs would be a whole lot easier" since *Maury* employees devote "hours and hours" to checking out stories and finding ones that are both real and appropriate for the show.

When asked if the show is real, the host is just as adamant as the executive producer in insisting that it is. "Of course," Povich stoutly maintains. "This is not *Springer*. Jerry and I have known each other a long time and I love his honesty: He says his show is wrestling. My show is not wrestling. My show is for real and these people, we check them out. I operate like a newsroom. We have seven production teams and they look at these stories, they check them out back in their hometowns, they talk to their friends, they talk to their family members." Because of that background checking, it is unlikely that people can just fabricate tall tales for their proverbial fifteen minutes of fame on Povich's program.

Behind-the-Scenes Secrets | 155

Guests are prepared for their appearances. "We go over the questions they will be asked before they go onstage," producer Christine Ponzi states. Since it is likely a guest has not previously been onstage, *Maury* workers assure them that the fact that they were chosen means they can do it. "We try to give them confidence," Mike Boornazian relates. "We tell them to go out there and be themselves."

In an article entitled "My Tuesday with Maury," Alexandra Symonds wrote about a college experience in which she and other college students had the opportunity to take a tour of the *Maury* studio, attend tapings, and have a question and answer session with the host himself. She reported that there were some things she found to be unexpectedly false: "The bricks in the wall are fake" made of a "linoleum substance" and are blue although they "appear red under the lights." She also saw that the show kept "several racks of clothing" for its guests." Female guests in two different segments "wore the same maroon shell-and-shrug twinset."

However, on much more important points, Symonds realized "These people are real. The bricks may not be real, but the stories are." Synods was impressed by the reality of "the blind terror" on a mother's face when "she learned her guy wasn't the father."

At the same time, Symonds observed the guests being coached: "Throughout the six segments we saw, one producer squatted at the edge of the stage, furiously scribbling, cues on pasteboard: "GO OFF ON HER," one sign advised a guest's new girlfriend, and later, "THINK OF YOUR FATHER."

It seems likely that, while the stories featured are true, there may be a certain amount of exaggeration for dramatic purposes. For example, in this book's section on makeovers, a person was quoted who said the show encouraged the woman to look more conservative than she usually did and her man to appear more of a "wild man" than he generally did.

Writing for the Internet site Reddit, a contributor vouched for the reality of *Maury*: "A guy I work with was a regular on *Mau-*

ry." The co-worker had first appeared on a segment knowing his girlfriend was going to reveal a secret. That secret was that the child they were raising together might not be biologically his. The writer elaborated, "He's crying and they bring out the guy she cheated with." DNA tests proved neither the boyfriend nor the "other man" sired the child. The Reddit writer said the co-worker appeared on several *Maury* shows before the biological father was in fact discovered. Perhaps nothing supports the reality of *Maury* more fully than the messiness of reality itself.

However, once again, the question presents itself as to *why* guests take their most intimate concerns onto a television show. One reason is that they can get something that would usually cost a pretty penny without reaching into their own (often quite limited) pocketbooks. "A polygraph test is expensive," Paul Faulhaber says. "We give them free." Producer Mike Boornazian asserts, "Someone calls us because they want to know the truth."

The show also offers "after care" from professionals for its distressed guests. "We give them professional help after the show for which they don't have to pay," Faulhaber adds.

The *Maury* Workplace and Workweek

Povich works two days per week on *Maury*: three shows are taped on Thursday and two shows are taped on Friday. On both days, he starts work at about 6:45 a.m. and winds it up at about 2:30 p.m. Of course, as of this writing, Maury is at an age when most people are retired so he remarks, "At my age, I'm working enough."

There is considerable brain exercise for Povich in researching his show. Matthew Trzcinski observes in *Screenrant*, "The octogenarian Maury Povich is nearly miraculously able to learn the personal details of between *30 and 40 guests per week*!" Povich believes the memorization needed to host his show may serve to work against one of the common terrors of aging and calls the memorization his "Alzheimer's check."

Maury is shot on the stage of the Stamford Center for the Arts. It is the same stage on which *The Jerry Springer Show* and *The Steve Wilkos Show* are shot. While Povich puts in two days a week to create *Maury*, Springer and Wilkos spend only one day a week to make their shows.

Interestingly, Jerry Springer frankly admits that he prefers Povich's program to his own, observing that *Maury* "deals with serious issues where we're a total circus. There's no redeeming social values in our show other than craziness." *No redeeming social values in our show other than craziness*? Since the "craziness" on Springer's program can hardly be seen as possessing "redeeming social value," it is obvious that Springer recognizes that there is simply nothing at all worthwhile about his show. He is honest about what he does and knows he puts out a lousy program that makes money because many people enjoy watching other people yell and tussle.

Safety is taken very seriously by *Maury*. About a dozen security guards—all of whom are off-duty police officers or firefighters—are on-site at all times when the program is being filmed. "If someone ever jumped onstage and rushed Maury, for example, that person would be in a headlock immediately by the security guards who are hidden amongst the audience members as well as stationed around the studio audience," Curt Ostermann notes. All *Maury* guests must pass through metal detectors like those that are standard in airports and are bodily searched to ensure no concealed weapons are brought onto the premises. Guests are escorted from dressing rooms and around the studio by security guards, Associate Producers, or both.

Celebrate! Celebrate! *Maury* is a Winner!

Beginning on April 28, 2016, and all through May 2016, *Maury* celebrated the fact that May 25 marked the 3,000th episode of the *Maury* show since it changed its format in 1998. In an interview with a journalist, Povich proudly proclaimed, "3,000 is not just a number to me, it's a big number."

NBC Broadcasting Chair Ted Harbert commented, "3,000 episodes is just more proof that Maury Povich is one of the most successful broadcasters in television history and all of us at NBC Universal hope he does 3,000 more."

As the celebration drew near, *Maury* Executive Producer Paul Faulhaber said, "It's been an honor and a privilege to work with Maury and our amazing creative staff for the past 18 years."

Just how would this milestone be celebrated? Toward the end of each new episode, a retrospective entitled "Top 30 of 3,000" was shown. These retrospectives showcased the most famous—or infamous—shows and the wildest and wackiest guests. Among those shown were Andrew with his "NOT the father" dance that went viral and the one-of-a-kind chicken tetrazzini show.

– 5 –
Maury Tragedies... Troubles... and a Toke

A show with countless fans and more than a few detractors, *The Maury Povich Show/Maury* became entangled with myriad troubles and at least a few genuine tragedies.

The *Maury* Link to Ayden Annes-Hensley's Tragically Brief Life

On the morning of November 16, 2005, a man in Lady Lake, Florida received a distressed phone call from his roommate, a

19-year-old woman named Samantha Preston. The man was Michael Willis, 24, who said of that call, "I couldn't even understand her." He thought her hysterical incoherence probably reflected "a state of shock."

Indeed it did. Preston had just realized that her baby, 2-month-old Ayden Annes-Hensley, was dead.

Only the day before this very untimely death, little Ayden had appeared on *Maury* because Preston and her live-in boyfriend, Robert Hensley, 24, wanted to learn whether Hensley or Willis was the biological father of Ayden. Since Preston and Hensley were a couple, it was Robert Hensley who acted as "daddy" to the infant. However, Preston, Hensley, and Willis knew that Willis had engaged in sex with Preston at about the time she was impregnated. Although Willis had not traveled to appear on the show, he cooperated with *Maury* representatives in providing a DNA sample. Willis felt confident of what the results would show. He told a *New York Post* journalist, "They went up there for the Maury Povich show to find out if it's Robert's son or mine" but added "I know it's my son" because the timing of conception had been when the mother "was with me."

When the couple appeared on *Maury*, Hensley heard, "You are NOT the father!" Willis, who was not present, was proved to have biologically sired Ayden.

When Preston and Hensley returned to the Upper West Side room at the Beacon Hotel that had been reserved for them by the show, they eventually got in bed—with the baby sleeping with them.

They woke up at about 6:00 a.m. to realize that little Ayden was not breathing! 911 was immediately called. Erika Martinez reported, "Ayden was taken by ambulance to Roosevelt Hospital, where he was pronounced dead on arrival."

Police searched the hotel room and questioned the couple. Neither Preston nor Hensley was charged with a crime. The baby appeared to have accidentally smothered to death.

Preston has two other children, one with Hensley and one with Willis. Both other kids were left in Florida.

"Our thoughts and prayers go out to the family," Povich commented, a statement of sympathy both simple and appropriate to the grim occasion.

Bianca Nardi's Allegations and Lawsuit

In 2006, *Maury* associate producer Bianca Nardi filed a $100 million sexual harassment lawsuit against the show. She was on medical leave from the show when she filed the suit. Defendants in the suit included Maury Povich himself, producer Donna Ingber, executive producer Paul Faulhaber, senior producer Vincent Fusco, Povich's company MoPo Productions, and NBC Universal Television. The suit charged she had been pressured to watch pornographic films and expose her body in such revealing garments as push-up bras, low-cut blouses, and short skirts. She also claimed to have been, in effect, barraged with sex-related remarks. Shortly after the suit was filed, Nardi's attorney, Bruce Baron, stated, "Many calls have been coming in both supporting and witnessing various conduct with respect to either [my client] or other employees who may have been afraid to come forward in the past."

A lovely blonde and occasional actress, Nardi started working for Povich after graduating from Syracuse University in 2000. In her suit, Nardi claimed that the working atmosphere took a turn for the worse when Povich began an adulterous affair with *Maury* producer Donna Ingber who was also married. *People* magazine stated, "Bianca Nardi, 28, of Fort Lee, N.J., says in court papers obtained by the Associated Press that the sexually charged atmosphere among the show's production staff was fostered by the 'intimate and sexual relationship between defendants Maurice Richard Povich and Donna Benner Ingber.'" *CNN.com* reported, "Nardi alleges that an affair between Povich and Engber, who is also married, afforded Engber special treatment that Faulhaber and Fusco resented. The two expressed their frustrations by sexually harassing Nardi and other women working for the show, the lawsuit states." According to Nardi, *Maury* executive producer Paul Faulhaber was upset by the liaison and took his frustrations out on Nardi by trying to get her involved with "alcohol, pornographic videos and parties inviting open and notorious sexual activities." Nardi contends Faulhaber pressured her to wear concealed cameras and microphones for undercover assignments in which she would do such things as venture into bars to catch married men propositioning her. She says such doings were outside her job description, but she complied for fear of being fired. *CBS News* reported, "Her lawsuit says that when she complained, Faulhaber retaliated by making her do other demeaning jobs." That same *CBS News* article also stated, "Court papers also say Nardi had an unfairly heavy workload because she did tasks that were supposed to be done by Ingber, who often refused to do her own work—without penalty—because of her relationship with Povich." Another Nardi allegation in court papers claimed Ingber, "many times in an intoxicated condition, telephoned [Nardi's] residence at all hours of the late evening to discuss her personal relations with defendant Povich (and other men whom she was secretly seeing) and would often ask Nardi what *Maury* staff were saying about her relationship with Povich. A *CNN.com* article reported that Nardi further alleged in the suit that "she was made to disrobe on tape and that the video was then shown in a New York City bar."

Nardi said she gained weight because of the stress of being sexually harassed and has required psychiatric treatment. "She was subjected to conduct that was unlawful and abusive," Baron maintained. "No one is above the law, no matter how powerful they think they are. Bianca is anxiously awaiting her day in court."

Maury spokesperson Gary Rosen denied Nardi's allegations. "We have done a complete and thorough investigation of her allegations of harassment and we are satisfied that there is no merit to them," Rosen stated. "We stand behind our experienced and dedicated staff, fully."

Rebecca Marks, a spokesperson for NBC, said, "We do not believe that Ms. Nardi was a victim of unlawful sexual harassment and intend to defend this lawsuit vigorously."

In early August 2006, New York State Supreme Court Justice Bernard Fried ruled that Bianca Nardi's claims of having suffered "sexually abusive and intimidating conduct" while working for *Maury* would be heard in closed-door arbitration rather than open court. He based it on an arbitration clause in Nardi's employment contract.

"We are confident an arbitrator will find her claims are without merit," said a *Maury* spokesperson.

Journalist Dareh Gregorian reported, "The ruling essentially brings a tepid end to a sensational lawsuit that included allegations

Povich was cheating on his wife with a show employee and that life backstage 'was permeated with the use of alcohol, pornographic videos and parties inviting open and notorious sexual activities." Nardi's suit claimed that *Maury* workers "published pictures of her breasts and used her recorded voice to accompany videotaped footage of a penis, and that both the pictures and the recording were shown on television programs and public bars."

2015: Another Dead Baby Tragedy

In March 2015, the parents of an 8-month-old baby traveled from Ohio to Stamford, Connecticut to appear on *Maury*. "Daddy" wanted to learn if his fatherhood was biological or not. On the very day, the family was scheduled to film a *Maury* episode, tragedy struck: they found the infant jammed between a mattress and a wall in the hotel room that the show had provided for the family. The baby was not breathing, apparently having suffocated to death. *NBC Connecticut* reported, "According to police, the 27-year-old mother woke up around 7 a.m. on Wednesday at the Stamford Plaza Hotel on Summer Street to find the baby on a pillow, unconscious and not breathing." The article continued that the mother told police "the baby must have fallen off the bed during the night and become lodged between the wall and the bed and called for help when she picked up the little girl and noticed she wasn't breathing." The "daddy," who may or may not have been the biological father, awakened to the mother's frantic screaming and supported her version of events when questioned by police.

A *Fox News* report stated that Stamford Police Lieutenant Diedrich Hohn "said the hotel was messy when the medics arrived and there were signs of a fight that took place in the hotel as food was thrown around the room as well as empty alcohol bottles. However, Hohn said the scene did not reveal an 'exorbitant' amount of alcohol."

The mom was 27 and dad was 25. The couple had a 2-year-old son and that child was in the hotel room but unharmed. *NBC Connecticut* reveals, "The baby was pronounced dead at Stamford Hospital. Her body was taken to the office of the chief medical examiner for an autopsy, which did not reveal what caused the infant's death, police said, but they ruled out physical abuse, sexual abuse, and neglect."

According to the *Stamford Advocate*, "A spokesperson for NBCUniversal extended her condolences to the family." That spokesperson, Janice Rosas, said, "On behalf of Maury and everyone at *The Maury Show*, we are deeply saddened by this profound tragedy. Our thoughts and prayers are with the family during this incredibly difficult time."

The Man From Middletown, Ohio Who Said "No!"

In September 2017, a Middleton, Ohio man filmed a police report against the *Maury* show alleging harassment. He made out a police report in which he alleged that *Mau-*

ry representatives made numerous phone calls to him and put multiple messages on his Facebook page. According to journalist Anya Wassenberg, "He claims the show approached him on Facebook, asking that he add their page. Then, he says one of the show's producers asked him about a relationship that he had been involved in many years prior. A young man claiming to be his son wanted an on-screen DNA test on the show. The man declined, but he says the show's reps continued to contact him. Then, a sibling of the alleged son filed a claim of sexual harassment against the same man." Truly, a tangled, but quintessentially *Maury*, situation!

The name of the man is Barry Moore. A *Cincinnati.com* piece quotes Moore as stating, "With the first message they sent me a message on Facebook and asked me to add them. I showed my wife and she said, "Hmm.' I said, 'I wonder what this is all about.'"

Moore was already aware that there was a man who thought Moore was his biological father. Moore felt pestered by *Maury* Facebook messages and telephone calls so he filed the aforementioned police report. According to *Cincinnati.com*, Moore says the phone calls only stopped "after he threatened to get a lawyer."

According to *Cincinnati.com*, the sibling's accusation was more serious than sexual harassment but was that Moore "sexually assaulted one of his kids 24 years ago when the child was three." The article states that Middletown Police are investigating the accusation of child molestation.

Moore agreed to pay for half the cost of a DNA test about the man who believed Moore was his father—but without appearing on *Maury*.

Povich Takes A Toke

Although Maury Povich frequently scolds the "wild teens" on his shows for getting high, he revealed in early 2019 on the radio show *Sway's Universe* that he had smoked a cigarette made of a special strain of marijuana named after his wife, Connie Chung! Povich shared that he had learned about the brand from comedian Lewis Black who was doing "a story on various marijuana [types] as they became legal, I think, in the state of Washington." It turned out that Connie Chung was also intrigued by the idea of a weed brand named after herself, so the wealthy and famous power-couple traveled to the state of Washington just to sample it. Commenting on her namesake pot strain, Chung wryly remarked, "I'm very easy to grow, I require less attention and care, and I give good yield. I'm perfect for daytime use when facing deadlines, and [people] need to be alert and imaginative."

– 6 –

Condemnation and Praise For an American Institution

Maury has garnered its share of criticism over the many years of its existence. It has been widely faulted as the nadir of "trash TV" and blasted from varied perspectives.

Criticism

Whitney Matheson writes a weekly column entitled *Pop Candy* in which she discusses popular culture. She began one such column with a take-off on the trademark Povich sign-off: "There shouldn't be a next time, America." She continues that *Maury* is well overdue for cancellation, writing, "Povich's show is, without a doubt, the worst thing on television." Matheson contends, "*Maury* is much further down the commode than *Jerry Springer* or *Jenny Jones*" because *Maury* pretends to be "a respectable, caring program." That pretense outrages Matheson and not a few others. She is also offended by the show's "focus on children," finding troubled teen episodes especially distasteful. What's more, Matheson believes cancellation would do the host "a gigantic favor." She believes, "When a tearful teen mama races offstage and out the back door, you get the sense he wants to follow her and never look back."

One area that tends to occasion critical comment has to do with the racial make-up of the guests. They are white, African-American, and Hispanic. There are very few Asian guests. It would be easy to make a joke about Povich's wife, Connie Chung, not wanting to watch her ethnic compatriots embarrass themselves on

TV. However, it seems more likely that certain cultural traditions tend to keep members of Asian-American communities from airing their troubles on TV—although there are undoubtedly some Asian *Maury* guests.

The heavy representation of African-Americans has led some commentators to fear the show plays upon negative racial stereotypes of that community. Writing for *The Root*, Shirea L. Carroll complains, "Since 1998, [the show has] been serving up the same old, same old as black folks line up in droves to humiliate themselves on TV." She also asserts, "While there isn't any data on the ratio of black mothers to white mothers searching for the fathers of their children, from what I've seen of the show, there are way too many young black mothers who don't know their baby's fathers" and speculates "with the number of black single mothers shown it would seem producers feel black single mothers make for better TV."

Mayukh Sen published a piece in *Topic* that discusses televised paternity testing and takes *Maury* to task for racial and class reasons. Sen notes, "Paternity segments also have a way of exposing the racial enmity that's prevalent in America as well as the gulfs between socioeconomic strata and the moral expectations placed on women with multiple partners." Sen quotes from Patricia Hill Collins, who wrote in her 2004 book, *Black Sexual Politics: African Americans, Gender, and the New Racism*, "Mr. Povich presents Black women and Black men in an especially stark light." Collins complains that his show plays on the racist stereotype of the "black deadbeat dad" and that by "showing the African American woman whose sexuality was so out of control that she had no idea who fathered her child, Mr. Povich panders to longstanding societal beliefs about Black sexuality."

One problem with the accusation of racism is that there is no lack of white guests on *Maury* and with the same problems his black and Hispanic guests have. Sen suggests that Caucasian women searching for the fathers of their babies are implied on the show to be "white trash" who are "doing poorly in life." Sen further argues that *Maury* guests—this criticism presumably covers those of all ethnic backgrounds—"exist within a contextual vacuum, absent of any structures that may have contributed to their plight." Nevertheless, Sen admits that Povich himself does *not* express contempt for women doing paternity tests but says, "I give them a lot of credit. And I'm only hoping and praying that those kids have a good life, even if it's with a single mother." However, Sen derides these sentiments as "paternalistic."

A contributor to a website called *Feministing.com* derides *Maury* as "one of the most sexist shows on television." The writer is especially critical of shows featuring "wild teen girls," noting that while some of them have engaged in illegal behavior such as truancy, unlawful drug use, and assault, "Some of them just have sex." The complainer continues that adolescent females who just had sex are sent on the program to a women's prison to "get yelled at by inmates and spend some time in solitary confinement." Such young ladies are not criminals, but they may well be *victims* of crimes if their sexual partners are adults. Thus, the show often appears to punish the victim while ignoring the actual perpetrator of a crime. The *Feministing* writer concludes: "If *Maury* made the laws, statutory rape would be a crime for the underage victim. If *Maury* made the laws, having unprotected sex would warrant a prison sentence."

While the *Feministing* contributor faults *Maury* for anti-female sexism, there are people who see it as having anti-male sexism. The Internet Movie Database (IMDb) has a "user review" section to which anyone may contribute. One such reviewer wrote "there seems to be an anti-male vibe" to the paternity episodes "with the man made to look like scum whether they are the fathers or not. In fairness, some men right from the start come off as decent (and the audience does show their approval of them), and the men who insult the women certainly aren't being forced to do so. Still, you sense a lot of bias."

Another IMDb user reviewer is even stronger in accusing the show of "relentless male bashing." That commentator believes paternity episodes make "the women seem like the innocent victims and the men pure evil at least 95% of the time."

Writing about *Maury* for *The New York Times*, Jeff Macgregor asks, "What's all the shouting about?" Then Macgregor answers his own question: "The shouting is about shouting, actually, because 'Maury' has bootstrapped itself into the American brainpan by making volume a virtue and battling evil at the top of its lungs." He faults the show for its "fig leaf of moral reclamation" while trading in "creepy titillations."

Plaudits for an American Pop Culture Institution

Although verbal brickbats are often hurled at *Maury*, there are some who stick up for the wildly popular program. An IMDb user review states, "Maury Povich treats his visitors with greater tact and gentleness than any of the others (except, perhaps, Oprah)." The writer acknowledges that he deals with people in dire situations that are often to some degree of their own making. However, there is more to his show, "With great sensitivity, he interviews people whose lives have taken an incredible turn… Through all of this, Maury treats his guests with the utmost courtesy and seems to wholly empathize with them."

A writer calling herself "Awesomely Luvvie" headlines a cheerfully sarcastic column, "The Maury Povich is a National Treasure." Luvvie says she "just wanted to do an ode to one of the funniest, most foolery-filled shows on television." She believes "Maury is unfuggwitable because he is an enabler of shenanigans."

On the TV.com website, a *Maury* fan wrote, "I like the Maury show because it has good variety and the people that are on his show have the need to get answers. The Maury show also has individuals that cause one to

Condemnation and Praise | 185

ask questions that hit home." Another TV.com contributor declared, "I love the show and I've been watching it for a long long time. My favorite shows are the Maury kids, the DNA testing and the man or woman shows. I love the show so much that I'm trying to get my son on the Maury kids because he loves to dance. So be on the lookout for my son because he will be on the next Maury kids hopefully. I love Maury and all that he does. He is really a blessing to those people who have no one else to turn to keep doing what you are doing Maury and I love you." Still another contributor to the same website wrote, "I would be upset if it was taken off air. It gives me something to look forward to every day. I watch the re-runs because sometimes it reminds me of how things are in the world. I hope that everyone learns something from watching the show. I've learned a lot about the world and how other people have it harder than others."

It may be a telling sign of just how much a part of popular culture *Maury* has become that it has been the subject of at least one

Master's dissertation. In that dissertation, American Studies graduate student Robyn Elizabeth Markarian states, "I believe it has given a forum that lets marginalized groups and 'ordinary' (in the sense that they are not already celebrities or have appeared on television before) people, a public soap box unavailable to them elsewhere in their lives."

One unquestionably biased admirer of Maury Povich is his equally famous wife, newscaster Connie Chung. "He's such a quick study," she comments. "It's very, very annoying. I observe him up close, at home, and then I watch his program and I don't really know how he does it. It comes so easily to him. It comes so easily to him, he doesn't take any notes." Chung continues that her own learning style is quite different: "I have always, over the years, worked so hard—hours and hours—and I take notes, I underline, and I think about what I'm doing, and he doesn't have to do that. And I really get annoyed."

Maury has no more dedicated fan than the host himself who shrugs off criticism of his program. "I like to do it," Povich asserts. "I think we do some good. I think we bring families together." He continues that friends of Povich who are, in his words, "so-called legitimate news" journalists will sometimes say, "You know, Maury, you were a great newsman. You were a great anchor. You could have gone back and done great stuff."

His reply? "I *am* doing great stuff," he asserts. "I'm fine with myself. I've no qualms about how everything turned out." Apparently, Whitney Matheson is wrong in her perception that Povich would like to run out of his studio and never look back.

When journalist Bryan Curtis inquired about "waking nightmares," the cheerful Povich answered, "No. *No*. I sleep well at night and my wife gives me great comfort. Ha ha ha…"

To many people, Povich is a kind of TV uncle or even Dad, a perception that pleases him. "I'm proud [that[… either through instinct or just basic human considerations, my guests and my viewers have kind of felt that

I was part of their family even though they know and I know that my experience in life is probably nothing [like what] they've gone through," he comments.

Maury is perennially relevant for its focus on the basics of human foibles, Povich believes. "When it comes to human instincts, do we ever really change?" he rhetorically asks. "Haven't we always had sensitivities? The only difference to me in terms of what we like to watch or what we think about ourselves is that more of it is out in public than it used to be." By contrast, "Now, everything is talked about." He points to the importance people often put on watching his program: "I have people writing me from college saying, 'I plan my classes around your show.'"

Brian Unger, who has worked on *Maury*, has said about Povich, "He is very paternal. I think that quality comes through in his television personality. He is going to get to the bottom of it. He's going to do it in a fair way with a sense of humor. And he's not going to judge anyone. Maybe that's what he is. He's

Condemnation and Praise | 189

everybody's daytime dad." Of course, as a "everybody's daytime dad," he need not share everyone's DNA!

The crew of *Maury* is made up of people who tend to be highly paid and to enjoy their jobs. As Curt Ostermann asserts, "Working on a show for several decades means working with the same people for years and years. We see and work with these people more than our own families. A ten-hour day in the studio is not uncommon. Consequently, all of us at the studio have all become a family, watching the younger people get married, have kids, and then hearing about those kids graduating from college and getting married themselves. Some of my best friends that I made at the studio have passed away, and other people come in to replace them, and then they become close friends. The family aspect of a hugely popular show that has as long a run as *Maury* is probably the most significant and enjoyable part of the job." At the time this author interviewed him, Oysterman had just had his 67th birthday. He intends to work on

Maury as long as it is possible. "I never plan to retire," he cheerfully declares. "I LOVE my job at *Maury* because of the people involved in the everyday production of the show. I miss those people when I am away from the studio, and I so look forward to returning to work each day that I am required to be there. I am so lucky to have this job!"

There is more than a hint of Liberace's reaction to negative reviews in his early career in Povich's stance. After a bad review of his performance, Liberace said, "I cried all the way to the bank." That sarcastic quip soon entered the lexicon. Povich told a story about playing golf with CBS analyst Gary McCord. "Maury, I've watched your show," McCord said. "I wouldn't do that show for $5 million a year!"

"Neither would I," Povich the fabulously wealthy super-earner cheekily replied. *Celebrity Net Worth* has reported that Povich is worth a staggering $60 million and receives an annual salary of $14 million.

Love him or hate him, criticize him or praise him, Maury Povich and his *Maury* program are an enduring part of America's popular culture. The public continues to enjoy the spectacles of *Maury* and, as long as they do, there will be a next time, America!

Bibliography

For allowing me to interview them for this book, the author extends her warmest thanks to Sherman Alpert, Robert Shearn, Susan Anton, Ray DeFeis Sr., Boris Cherniak, Andrew Basemen, Pam Porter, Kathy Garver, Courtney Blackmore, and Spyros Poulos.

"1975 J. G. Taylor Spink Award Winner Shirley Povich." National Baseball Hall of Fame.

"8-month-old baby found dead before parents were reportedly set to appear on 'Maury Show.'" *Fox News*. March 14, 2015.

Baldwin, Michael. "Middletown man files harassment complaint against the Maury Show." *Cincinnati.com*. Sept. 28, 2017.

Berkow, Ira. "Shirley Povich Dies at 92: Washington Sports Columnist." *The New York Times*. June 7, 1998.

Brannon, Jake. "12 People Share Their Stories on How Things Really Work TV Shows Like 'Maury' and 'Jerry Springer.'" humansoftumblr.com

Busy, Kelli. "My Worst Nightmare Lunch with Coworkers and the 'Maury Show—Man or Woman?'" *Planet Transgender*. 9/17/2019.

Carroll, Shirea L. "Why Is 'Maury Povich' Still On The Air?" *The Root*. 4/8/10.

Crews, Chip. "Paternity Ward Cross 'Maury' With a DNA Test and What Do You

Get? Big Ratings." *The Washington Post*. March 28, 2006.

Curtis, Bryan. "From Here to Paternity." *Grant and*. Nov. 8, 2013.

Fisher, Jim. "The Polygraph Wars." http://jimfisher.edinboro.edu/forensics/polywar1.html

Gregorian, Dareh. "Icing on the 'Rake'—Sex-Booze Accuser Partied with Maury." *New York Post*. April 26, 2006.

Gregorian, Dareh. "Maury Suit Slam - Sent To Arbitration." *New York Post*. Aug. 4, 2006.

"If Maury Made the Laws." *Feministing.com*. 3/11/2009.

Luvvie, Awesomely. "The Maury Povich Show is a National Treasure." awesomelyluvvie.com. June 26, 2015.

Macgregor, Jeff. "Saving the World, One Sexy Teen at a Time." *The New York Times*. July 16, 2000.

Margarin, Robyn Elizabeth. "'You Are Not The Father!': Family, Blood, Race, and Maury in America." *Dissertations, Theses, and Masters Projects*. Paper 1539626705.

Mathewson, Whitney. "Pop Candy." *USA Today*. 3/12/2002.

"Maury (1991-). Full Cast & Crew." *Internet Movie Database*.

"Maury Povich Biography." *Internet Movie Database*.

"Maury Talks Accuracy Of Lie Detector, Past Relationship w/Donald Trump + More." https://www.youtube.com/watch?v=B73QFJ44IBM&t=408s

"Motivational Hypnotist as seen on Maury." *Comedy wood.blogspot.com*. Aug. 21, 2008.

Nickerson, John. "Deceased baby's parents were to do Maury Povich show paternity test." *Stamford Advocate*. March 12, 2015.

"On the next Maury: Porn, booze, affairs claims." *CNN.com*. April 25, 2006.

Parents in Baby Hotel Death Case Came for Paternity Test on 'Maury Show.'" *NBC Connecticut*. March 13, 2015.

"Polygraph/Lie Detector FAQs." International League of Polygraph Examiners. http://www.theilpe.com/faq_eng.html

"Povich Sued For Sexual Harassment." *CBS News*. April 25, 2006.

Rawden, Jessica. "The Most Shocking Paternity Reveal In The History Of Maury, According To Maury." *Cinemablend.com*.

Rudolph, Christopher. "Manila Luzon And William Live A '90s Talk Show Fantasy In 'That's A Man, Maury.'" *NewNowNext*. 7/14/2017.

Sen, Mayukh. "Who's Your Daddy?" *Topic.com*. Issue No. 12.

Silverman, Stephen M. "Maury Povich in $100 Million Sex Lawsuit." *People*. April 25, 2006.

Skulk, Liz. "Maury show producer says 80-year-old talk show 'daddy' isn't slowing down." *Stamford Advocate*. May 13, 2016.

"Stop Exploiting Transgender Women!" *Change.org*

Synods, Alexandra. "My Tuesday with Maury." *Columbia Spectator*. March 27, 2013.

"The Maury Povich Show." TV.com

To, Katherine. "Lie Detection: The Science and Development of the Polygraph." https://illumin.usc.edu/lie-detection-the-science-and-development-of-the-polygraph/

"The Truth About Lie Detectors (aka Polygraph Tests). American Psychological Association. https://www.apa.org/research/action/polygraph

Trzcinski, Matthew. "25 Bizarre Behind the Scenes Details About Maury." *Screenrant*. May 5, 2019.

Walkman, Allison J. "Connie Chung Offers Personal View of Maury Povich." *TV Week*. Sept. 30, 2007.

Washington Post Staff compilation. "Shirley Povich's Biography." *The Washington Post*. Oct. 15, 1997.

Wassenberg, Anya. "15 Dirty Secrets Producers Don't Want You To Know About The Maury Show." *The richest.com*. Nov. 3, 2017.

"You Are NOT the Father!" *Know Your Meme*.

www.ingramcontent.com/pod-product-compliance
Lightning Source LLC
LaVergne TN
LVHW051518070426
835507LV00023B/3175